SUPER
Book of
Arts and Crafts

Written by
Adrianne Gant
Laurie Kastorff
Linda Milliken

Illustrations
Barb Lorseyedi

Typography
Lorraine Stegman
Caryn Steichen

TABLE OF CONTENTS

SUPER BOOK OF ARTS & CRAFTS

Planning Notes

To make your planning easier you will find the following information and ideas:

Things You'll Need
At a glance you'll know what to prepare. Materials required appear in a box or in bold type.

Art Start
Spark student interest before you begin the art lesson. Plan a pre-art lesson using the suggested activities.

Technique Tip
Follow these simple suggestions to increase student success and improve art technique.

Holiday Help
Learn more about holiday celebrations and traditions.

Artistic Fact
Interesting information about art to share with students. Students will develop an appreciation for and understanding of the world of art and art history.

Followup Fun
The project is complete...try these activities to extend the learning experience

SUPER BOOK OF ARTS & CRAFTS

Planning Notes

Display
Creative suggestions for displaying student artwork in the classroom. Display all projects and increase self-esteem. Develop the concept that *all* art is a success.

Variations, Idea Menu
Loads of ways to adapt a technique or project idea to year-round activities. Prefaced with a holiday-related symbol, you'll know in a glance if there's an idea to use for a specific holiday.

🍁	Fall Harvest	❤	Valentines Day
❄	Winter:	☘	St. Patricks Day
✿	Spring	🐇	Easter
✵	Summer	👑	Victoria Day
🎃	Halloween	✷	Fourth of July
🌽	Thanksgiving		Presidents' Day
🌲	Christmas	🏳	Flag Day

Index
Located in the back of the book. Need a specific holiday, theme, quick-and-easy project or technique? Look it up in the index.

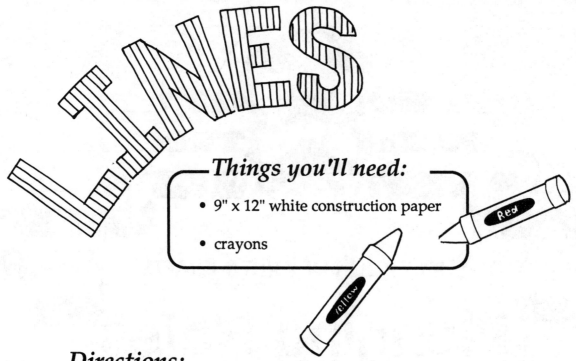

LINES

Things you'll need:

- 9" x 12" white construction paper
- crayons

Directions:

1. Make the outline of a picture with black crayon.
2. Fill in each section with parallel or curved lines. The lines can follow the shape of the object.
3. Every section should be a different color.

Variation:

- Younger students can draw a design instead of a picture.
- Draw a colorful dyed egg—pretty enough for the Easter Bunny.

DOTS & DESIGNS

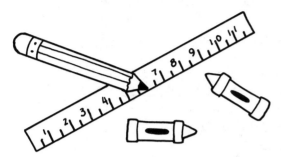

Things you'll need:

- one 9" x 12" white construction paper
- pencil • ruler • crayons
- felt pen or colored pencil

Directions:

1. Put a dot smaller than a penny anywhere on the paper.
2. Use the ruler and pencil to draw *seven* lines that radiate from the dot out to the edges of the paper.
3. Put a second dot anywhere on the paper.
4. Draw *five* lines that radiate from that dot to the edges of the paper.
5. Color each section with a different design.

TRACINGS

Things you'll need:

- white construction paper
- school scissors
- pencil
- crayons

Directions:

1. Trace scissors onto white paper, overlapping them to make a design.

2. Scissors can be opened, closed or a combination of positions.

3. Color in the spaces created by the overlapping lines with either blue, purple and green crayon or orange, yellow and red crayon.

Variation:
• Try tracing other classroom objects such as paintbrushes or rulers.

SUPER BOOK OF ARTS & CRAFTS • Edupress • ©1990

Disguised Letters

Things You'll Need:

- white construction paper
- manuscript letter patterns
- crayons

Directions:

1. Pass out manuscript letter patterns at random to students.

2. Trace letter on the white paper.

3. Color a picture using the letter as part of the picture.

SOAP & CRAYON MELT

THINGS YOU'LL NEED

- soap flakes (**Ivory** is suggested)
- waxed paper
- water
- plastic containers
- crayons
- vegetable peeler or cheese grater
- newspaper
- iron

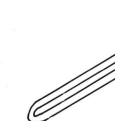

Directions

1. Have water in a plastic tub nearby.
2. Mix a small amount of water with soap flakes on top of a piece of waxed paper.
3. Move the flakes around to make a picture, write your name or draw shapes.
4. Add crayon shavings to the picture.
5. Place a sheet of waxed paper over the top. Iron to melt the crayon.
6. Cut the finished product into an animal, plant, number, letter or other imaginative shape.

Technique Tip

Set the iron to "wool" setting. Do not iron directly on the waxed paper. Place a sheet of newspaper between.

Adjust the iron's temperature if necessary.

Stuffed Crayon Shapes

Things You'll Need:

- white butcher paper
- crayons
- diluted tempera paint
- yarn and decorations
- newspaper • stapler

Directions:

1. Draw a large shape on a piece of doubled white butcher paper.

2. Cut out the shape. (You should have two.)

3. Use crayon to color the **opposite** sides of the shape heavy and solid.

4. Crunch up both pieces. Lay flat again. Wash with tempera, any color.

5. Stuff the shape with newspaper and staple shut.

6. Decorate if you choose.

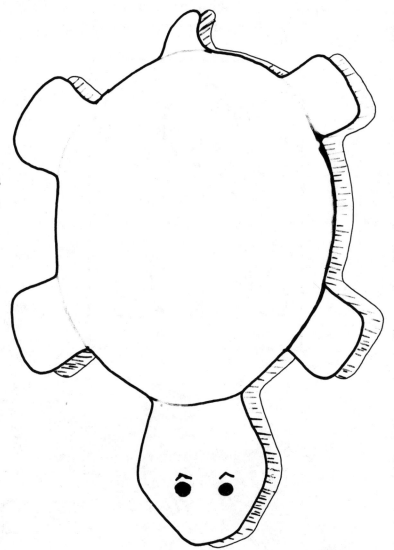

PATCHWORK PUZZLE

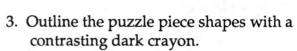

Things you'll need:

- one 9" x 12" white construction paper
- one 9" x 12" black construction paper
- puzzle pattern (following)
- pencil • crayons
- scissors • glue

Directions:

1. Reproduce puzzle pattern on white paper.
2. Sketch a simple picture over the puzzle then outline heavily with dark crayon.

3. Outline the puzzle piece shapes with a contrasting dark crayon.
4. Cut out the puzzle pieces.
5. Color each piece individually—solid, stripes, dots and so on—changing the design each time you reach a new line. Each piece will be different!
6. Reassemble the puzzle on black paper and glue in place.

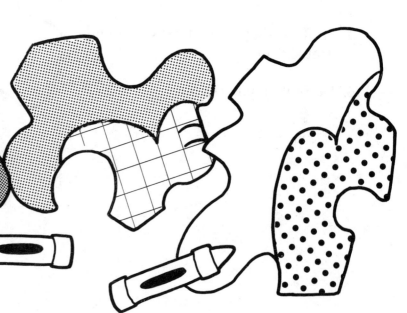

Jack-in-the Box

Here's an "artsy" lesson in shapes.

Things You'll Need:

- 9" x 12" construction paper
- assorted colors construction paper
- glue • scissors • crayon

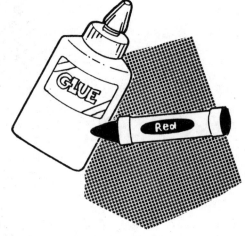

Directions:

1. Cut these shapes from construction paper—one triangle, one circle, six rectangles—each shape should be a different color.

2. Assemble the shapes as shown—and glue to construction paper background.

3. Add a crayon face.

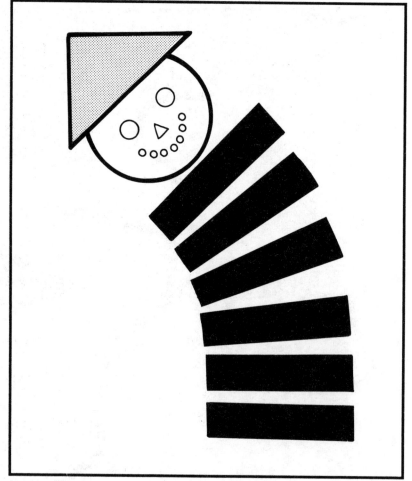

Clownin' Around

Directions:

1. Fold the paper in half, lengthwise. Draw a half body against the fold. Cut out along the outline.

2. Use a variety of material to make a clown suit. Add silly shoes and a huge necktie.

3. Glue yarn hair, mouth and eyes.

Display:
Cut a huge "big top" tent for the classroom wall. Tack the colorful clowns inside and around the big top.

Geometric Lockup

Things You'll Need:

- construction paper
- ruler
- scissors
- glue
- compass
- pencil

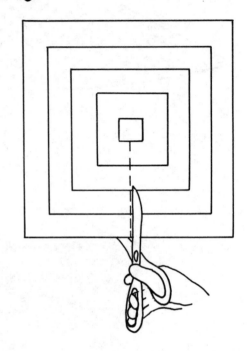

Directions:

1. Draw a large geometric shape on construction paper.

2. Measure 1/2 inch (1.25 cm) inside the original shape and repeat the drawing.

3. Continue this procedure until the center of the paper is reached.

4. Make a cut from one edge to the center (as shown by the dotted lines).

5. Cut out all the geometric shapes.

6. Arrange in an interlocking design on a large sheet of paper and glue in place.

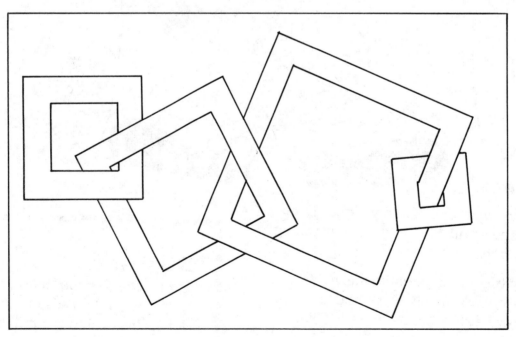

Start with a

Things You'll Need:

- construction paper circle, any size and color
- 9"x12" white construction paper for background
- paste • crayons

Directions:

1. Paste the circle to the white paper.

2. Complete a picture using crayons. The circle should be part of the picture.

Guardian Angel

Display Ideas

Hang this angel over your desk and you'll feel like you always have a friend who cares.

Things You'll Need:

- angel pattern (following)
- variety of colored construction paper
- scissors • glue • pencil
- glitter, lace, ribbon (optional)

Directions:
1. Trace and cut pattern pieces from colored paper. Be sure you have cut:
   1 body
   2 arms
   1 head
   4 hands & feet
   1 wing
2. Assemble and glue angel together as shown below.
3. Add construction paper detail and trim.
4. Add optional trim.
5. Hang with yarn.

Followup Fun

Write a story about an adventure you had with your guardian angel.

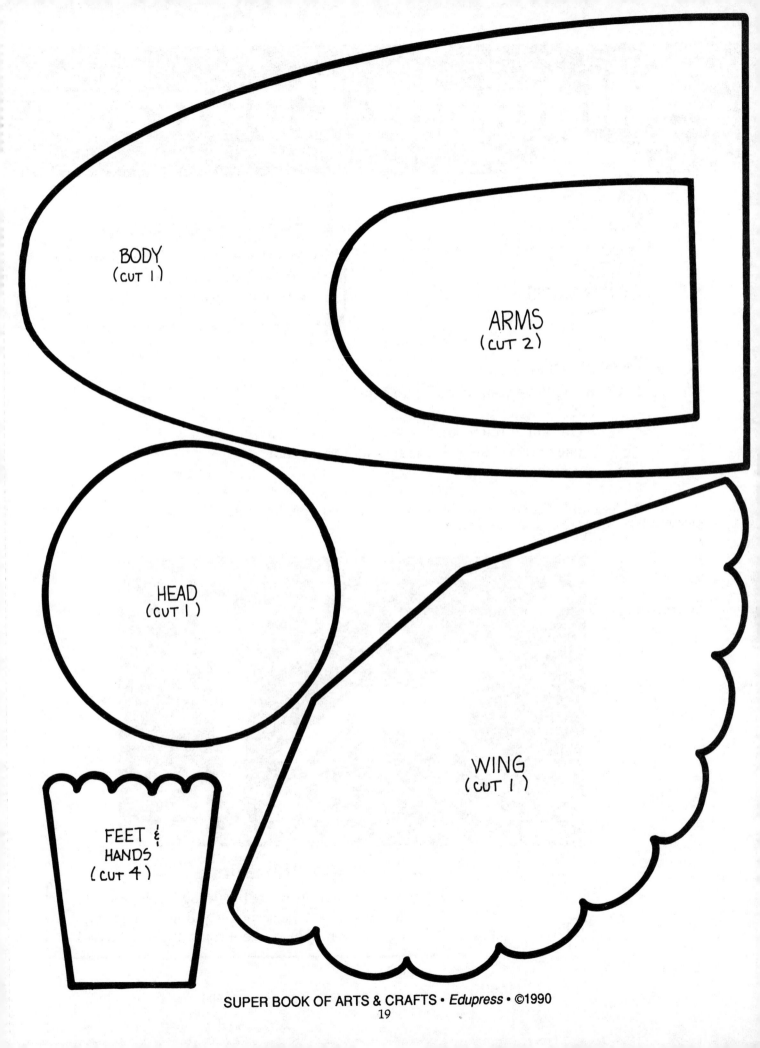

BODY
(CUT 1)

ARMS
(CUT 2)

HEAD
(CUT 1)

WING
(CUT 1)

FEET &
HANDS
(CUT 4)

Midnight Contrast

Things You'll Need:

- 9"x12" black construction paper
- white construction paper
- scissors   • glue

Directions:

1. Cut a nighttime scene from white paper.
   Include:
   - crescent or full moon
   - one or two simple objects such as a tree or house
   - ground covering

2. Assemble the shapes on black construction paper and glue in place.

Variations:

- Make a daytime scene by gluing black on white.
- Make a color-tone scene by gluing a warm color (red or orange) to a cool color (blue or purple).

E-x-p-a-n-d-a-b-l-e Design

Things You'll Need:

- 12" x 18" construction paper
- 6" x 9" construction paper, contrasting color
- glue
- scissors

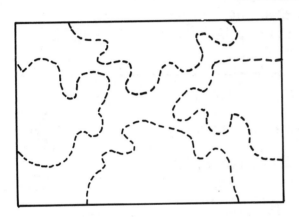

Directions:

1. Draw a "jigsaw" shape on each side of the 6" x 9" paper.

2. Cut out each sketched shape and save.

3. Glue the remaining section of the 6" x 9" paper to the **center** of the large paper.

4. Match the cut out shape to its original position. Flip it to its reverse side, as if the pieces were being folded out. Glue in position.

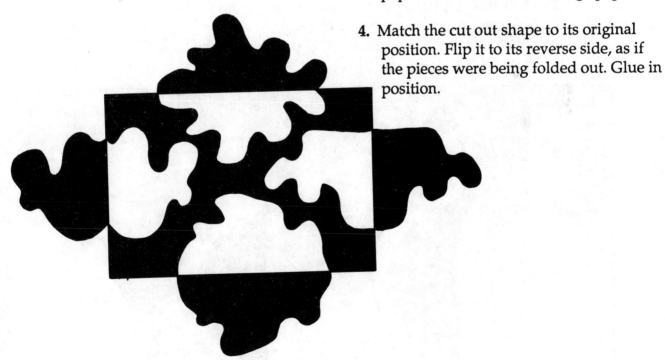

Penguins on Parade

Things you'll need:

- construction paper in various sizes and colors:
  - one 12" x 18" light or royal blue
  - one 9" x 12" white
  - one 6" x 6" black
  - one 6" x 6" orange
- black crayon • white chalk • glue
- compass or circle patterns (following)

Directions:

1. Trace and cut these circles. Older students can practice using a compass to make the circles.
   - 2 - 2" orange, each cut in half—feet and beaks
   - 2 - 3" white—heads
   - 1 - 5" black, cut in half—flippers
   - 1 - 6" white, cut in half—body
2. Use black crayon to outline icebergs on the blue background.
3. Color the icebergs with white chalk.
4. Follow the illustration to glue two penguins to the background.

Penguin Pattern

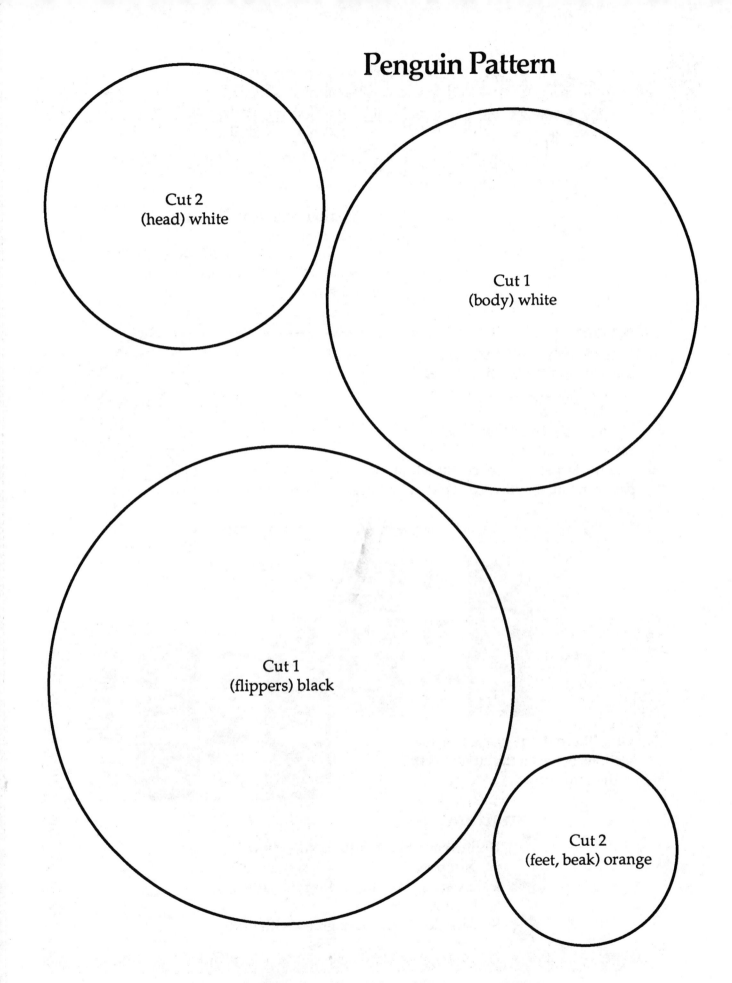

Cut 2
(head) white

Cut 1
(body) white

Cut 1
(flippers) black

Cut 2
(feet, beak) orange

Repeated Patterns
Repeated Patterns
Repeated Patterns

Things you'll need:

- 9" x 12" construction paper, any color
- two 3" x 9" contrasting color papers
- scissors • glue

Directions:

1. Place the two smaller pieces of construction paper on top of each other. Fold in half lengthwise.
2. Cut shapes along the folded edge leaving a space between each shape. Save the small shapes.
3. Fold the larger piece of construction paper in half lengthwise. Fold in half again. Unfold and lay flat on the table.
4. Glue the cut paper panels to alternate sections of the flat paper.

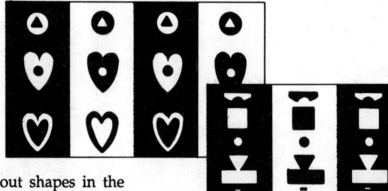

5. Glue the cut-out shapes in the sections between the cut panels in the same order.

Variations:

 Halloween: Black with orange cut-out pumpkins

 Valentine's Day: Red with pink cut-out hearts

 St. Patrick's Day: Dark green with lime green cut-out shamrocks

WAVY WEAVING

THINGS YOU'LL NEED:

- two 9"x12" construction paper, contrasting colors
- scissors • ruler
- glue • pencil

DIRECTIONS:

1. On one piece of construction paper, measure and draw a pencil line the width of the paper, one inch (2.5 cm) from one end. Cut four wavy lines **up to** the pencil line.

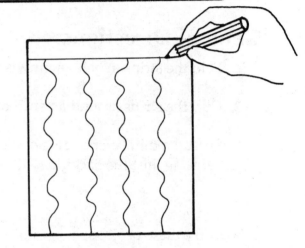

2. Cut six wavy lines, one at a time, across the width of the second piece of paper.

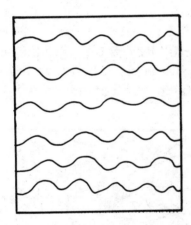

3. Weave the strips through the first piece of paper.

4. Glue down all the ends and trim the edges.

VARIATION:

Use colorful magazine pictures instead of construction paper.

Curled Paper Projects

Once you've learned the technique of curling paper you can
make a variety of appealing art projects!

Things You'll Need:

- construction paper strips, 1" (2.5 cm) x varying lengths and colors
- scissors
- glue
- construction paper for backing

General Directions:

1. Fold the strips in half lengthwise.

2. Curl the strips around a pencil or any other cylinder shape.

3. Spread a thin layer of glue on the backing paper. glue the curled strips in place, folded edge against the backing.

Now try these projects:

Freeform Curls

Glue curled shapes of varying tightness against a colorful background. Try this as a cooperative, small group project. Use colors suitable for seasons or holidays, if you wish. Older children can create shades from left to right on the paper. Begin with red on the left and finish with pale pink on the right for example.

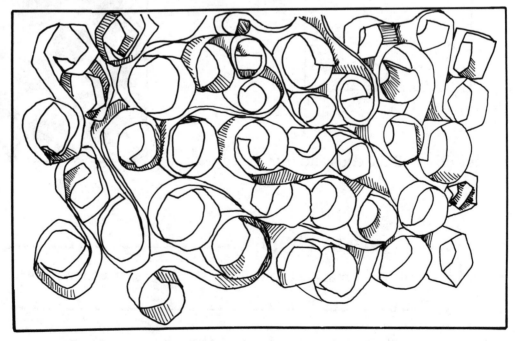

Curled paper can also be glued inside a border. To make the border, start with long strips of construction paper, glued together at each end to create a closed shape.

Try these:

Fish
Add some curled paper bubbles!

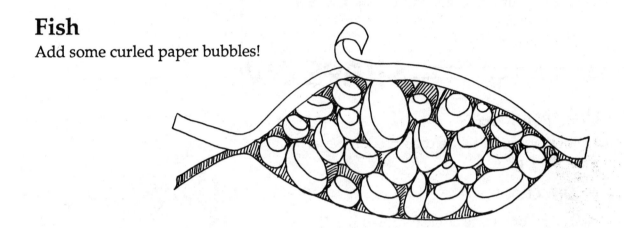

Fruit
Fill a cornucopia or talk about nutrition.

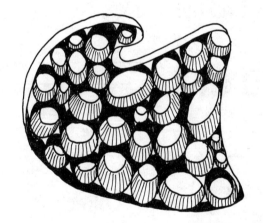

Kite
Add a crepe paper tail.

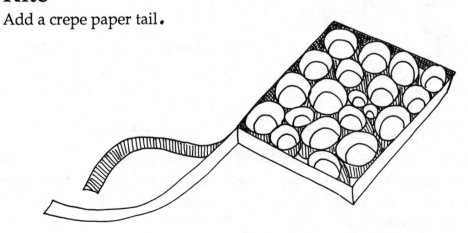

Wise as an OWL

Art Start

Talk about the expression "Wise as an owl." What is wisdom? Talk about wise choices.

Can students think of other animal expressions?
"Quick as a bunny."
"Sly as a fox."

SHAPE OWL

Things you'll need:

- yellow, brown & white construction paper
- scissors • glue

Directions:

1. Cut one large circle for the body. Cut two circles for the eyes plus two smaller circles for the eyeballs. Cut a triangle beak, beard, tail and hat. Cut two rectangle claws.

2. Assemble and glue together as shown.

WIDE-EYED OWL

Things you'll need:

- pattern, following
- muffin baking cups
- construction paper scraps
- scissors • glue

Directions:

1. Trace and cut out owl pattern from construction paper.
2. Glue bottoms of two muffin cups in place as shown.
3. Add cut paper eyes, beak and mouth.

On Display

Arrange owls on twisted shopping bag branches on the classroom wall. Add lettering, "Words of Wisdom from Room 22." Tack up a large sheet of butcher paper. Children write or dictate words of advice.

Sack Quack

— Things You'll Need: —

- paper sack
- string or yarn
- newspaper
- orange, yellow and black construction paper
- scissors • glue

Directions:

1. Crumple newspaper into two balls. Put the largest in the bottom of the paper sack and tie string around the bag just above the ball. Put the smaller newspaper ball in the sack above the string and fold the top of the bag over. Tape or staple to hold.

2. Cut:

    - two yellow wings

    - two orange feet

    - one orange beak.

    - two black eyes and lashes

3. Assemble and glue.

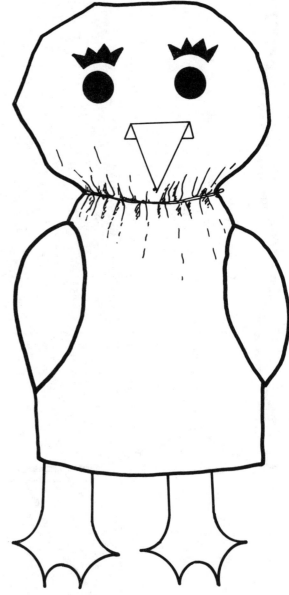

$\mathcal{W}\;\mathcal{A}\;\mathcal{V}\;\mathcal{E}\;\mathcal{S}$

Art Start

Discuss different kinds of waves—stormy, calm, rolling. Talk about the differences between waves in the ocean and lakes. Fill a large tub with water and have some fun creating different wave effects.

Before yo
air with
moving

Cut Paper Waves

1. Cut different "wavelike" patterns from varied colors of construction paper.

2. Overlap the strips and glue on a manila construction paper backing.

Easy Crayon Waves

1. Use crayons to draw different kinds of waves from left to right across the paper.

2. Color each area between the waves a different shade.

Fantastic Footprints

Things You'll Need:

- four 9"x12"(half sheets) construction paper (five different colors)
- one 12"x18"(full sheet) construction paper (different color than others)
- pencil • scissors • glue

Directions:

1. Take off your shoes and socks. Trace around your foot on FOUR half sheets of construction paper.

2. Cut out one footprint exactly as traced. (Keep both parts of the paper.) Cut out the remaining three footprints as follows:

   - 1/2" (1.25 cm) larger than the traced pattern.

   - 1" (2.5 cm) larger than the traced pattern

   - 1 1/2" (3.75 cm) larger than the traced pattern.

3. Assemble the footprints on the large sheet of paper. On one half, glue the actual print, largest to smallest, on top of each other. On the other half, glue the footprint frames, smallest cut out print to largest on top of each other. (See illustrations.)

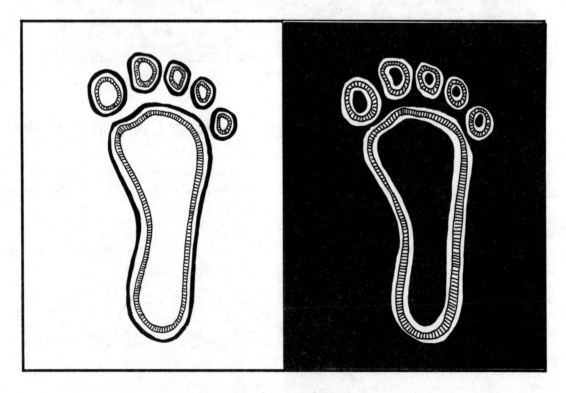

Ladybugs in the Grass

Directions:

1. Cut out long blades of grass from the two shades of green tissue. Lay along the bottom edge of the construction paper. The blades should overlap.

2. Cut three or more small ovals from the red tissue. Add black dots. Starch. Arrange among the blades of grass.

3. Starch in position to the background paper.

.... **Technique Tip** ....

Hold the tissue in place with one hand while you paint with the other.

Dilute the starch slightly.

Use the least amount of starch as possible.

WAYS WITH WATERCOLORS

SIMPLE SCENES

THINGS YOU'LL NEED:

- one 12"x18" white construction paper
- black crayon
- watercolors • brush
- tempera paint
- sponges

TECHNIQUE TIPS

Select **simple** shapes to outline.

This is a 2 day project.

DIRECTIONS:

1. Outline a simple scene with a pencil. Go over your outlines with black crayon.

2. Using watercolors, paint the scene, except for the background. Leave the background white. Let your picture dry.

3. Using a sponge, lightly dab a tempera background.

VARIATIONS:

 Christmas - stockings on a mantle

 Halloween - pumpkins on a fence

 Easter - eggs in the grass

 Summer - whales in the ocean

Wet on Wet

Wet a piece of **white paper**. Use **watercolors** to make a picture or design (flowers, fish, planes, etc.). Outline using black paint and allow to dry. Mount and hang.

Technique Tip

Fill a tub with water for speedier dipping of the paper. If the paper starts to dry, rewet with a spray bottle.

SUNSET WASH

THINGS YOU'LL NEED:

- white construction paper
- black construction paper
- watercolors • brush
- water containers
- small sponge • paste

DIRECTIONS:

1. Cover one side of the white paper with a water-soaked sponge. Stroke from one side to the other. Turn paper over and smooth down. Wet the top side of the paper the same way.

2. Fill the brush with purple paint. Start on one side, at the top, and pull the brush all the way across the paper.

3. Rinse brush and fill with red paint. Pull brush from one side to the other directly under the purple paint. Repeat with orange and then yellow paint.

4. Continue alternating bands of color to the bottom of the paper.

5. When dry, cut silhouettes out of black paper and paste over the top of the wash.

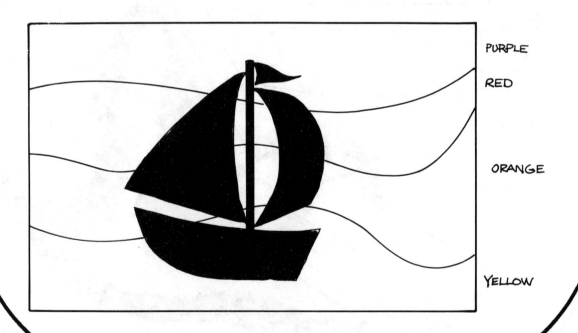

PURPLE

RED

ORANGE

YELLOW

FOLD AND DYE PAPERS

THINGS YOU'LL NEED:

- rice paper, silk span or paper towels
- watercolors

DIRECTIONS:

1. Fold paper as desired — accordion, radial, triangles, squares.

2. Saturate paper with water. Blot out excess water by pressing between paper towels.

3. Dip corners and edges into different colored paints. Refold the paper in many ways and redip. Unfold carefully.

4. After paper is dry it can be pressed with a warm iron and mounted to a colorful backing.

RUBBER CEMENT WASH

THINGS YOU'LL NEED:

- watercolors
- paint brush
- rubber cement
- 9"x12" white construction paper

DIRECTIONS:

1. Use rubber cement to draw a simple picture or design on white construction paper. Do not cover the whole paper. Let dry.

2. Apply a watercolor wash over the paper. Let dry.

3. Rub off the rubber cement. The designs and shapes or picture will have remained white.

4. You can repeat this process by putting rubber cement over different parts of the paper and applying another wash.

PRETTY FILTERS

Paint five or more round **coffee filters** with **watercolors**.
Paste filters in random positions to **colored construction paper**.

The filters can be flat or crumpled as children experiment.

VARIATION

After filters have dried, use markers to connect them in an interesting design on the paper background.

TECHNIQUE TIP

The brush must be fairly wet. Keep a container of water handy for frequent brush cleaning and wetting.

Try-it With Tempera

Spray Play

Things You'll Need:

- variety of spray bottles
- tempera paint
- water
- white drawing paper

Here are two variations using spray bottles and tempera paint. They should be done outdoors on a bright, sunny day!

➡ Drop "blobs" of paint on butcher paper. Vary the colors and size of the paint blobs. Fill the bottles with water and experiment with the nozzle. Spray the blobs from different distances and streams of water.

➡ Dilute the paint in the bottle of water. (Try a mixture of equal parts paint and water.) Spray paint a large sheet of butcher paper.

Try-it With Tempera

Paint that has been "pressed" takes on a variety of wonderful shapes and is always a special transformation for students to see. This is a successful project for any age. Try these two variations:

Folded Blobs

Fold a large sheet of *white construction paper* in half. Drop several blobs of *paint in assorted colors* along the fold.

Refold. Use your hand on the outside of the paper to squish the paint and move it away from the fold.

Open the paper. Allow to dry. Shapes can be cut out and mounted again on colorful paper or enjoyed as is.

Squished Paint

Make a paint "squisher" by punching a hole (use a *hammer* and *nail*) through the center of a *jar lid*.

Reinsert the nail through the lid. Cover the sharp end with masking tape. Tape the nail against the lid to hold it in place.

Use a plastic spoon to drop blobs of paint on a piece of white construction paper.

Hold the "squisher" by the nail end and press the flat lid against the paint blob. Squish and twist. Move the squisher to a new blob and repeat. Colors will mix and create interesting patterns.

Try-it With Tempera

Tempera Tracks

Collect an *assortment of boxes*—gift boxes (shirt, blouse), spirit master, and shoe boxes work especially well.

Cut *white paper* to fit the bottom of the box. Use a plastic spoon to drop five to seven paint spots around the paper. Color selection may vary. Use two to three colors.

Select a *tracking object* (see below), place it in the box and carefully tilt the box back and forth, side to side.

The object will roll around in the box and leave an interesting trail of colorful tracks.

Remove the paper, allow the paint to dry and mount on contrasting paper.

More than one tracking object may be used. *Don't overdo!*

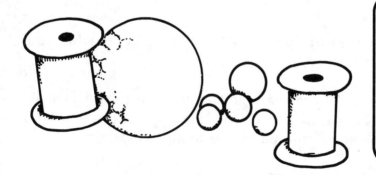

Tracking Objects

- marbles
- thread spools
- ping-pong balls
- golf ball

Try-it With Tempera
Spatter Painting

Things You'll Need:
- tempera paint
- construction paper
- stencil or pattern
- toothbrush (or similar)
- scotch tape

Directions:

1. Use the scotch tape to lightly secure the stencil or pattern to the construction paper.

(It doesn't matter whether a stencil or pattern is used—the effect will be the same.)

2. Dip the toothbrush into a shallow pan of paint. Hold the brush by the handle and gently shake it over the paper. (Be sure to cover the desks with newspaper first.)

More than one color of paint can be used.

3. When the paint has dried, remove the stencil or pattern.

Stencil

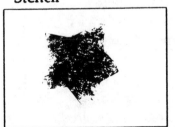

Pattern

Try-it With Tempera

Terrific Drips!

Things You'll Need:
- long sheet of butcher paper
- liquid detergent
- tempera paint; variety of colors
- masking tape
- wide-bristled paint brushes or foam brushes.

Go outside on a nice day for this project.

Directions:

1. Tape a long piece of butcher paper on a fence or wall.

2. Mix liquid detergent and tempera paint (about 4-1). Have a selection of several colors and a wide-bristle brush for each.

3. Dip the brush into the paint and press the bristles to the top of the paper. The paint should make a large "blob" where the brush was pressed, and then drip down the suspended paper.

4. Repeat with other colors, overlapping "blobs" and alternating colors.

Try-it With Tempera
Vaseline Prints

Things You'll Need:
- white construction paper
- vaseline
- powdered tempera paint
- cardboard tube or brayer
- piece of cardboard, as big (or bigger) than construction paper
- pencil

Directions:

1. Lightly sketch a pencil drawing of any object or holiday theme on white construction paper.

2. Mix 1 teaspoon vaseline with any color powdered tempera paint. Put the mixture in the center of the cardboard. Roll the mixture over the cardboard with a brayer or cardboard tube.

3. Place the drawing on the paint-covered cardboard with the drawing facing up.

4. Trace over the picture with a blunt object, like a crayon or craft stick.

5. Carefully pull off the picture and let dry.

6. Add a construction paper frame to match or accent the trempera used.

Try-it With Tempera
Bubble Prints

Things You'll Need:
- several small jars
- dish detergent • water
- tempera paint
- lightweight drawing paper
- straw

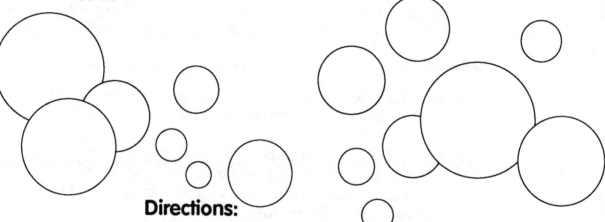

Directions:

1. Prepare several jars with a mixture of 4 tablespoons detergent, 1/2 cup water and 2 teaspoons tempera paint. Shake.

2. With a straw, blow gently into the mixture in each jar.

3. Place lightweight drawing paper over the bubbles. The bubbles will burst and leave a print. Overlap colors and bubbles.

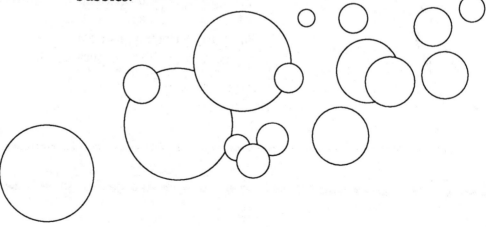

Powdered Tempera Tricks

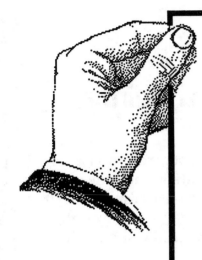

Hand Jive

Sprinkle several colors of *powdered tempera paint* over the surface of *lightweight drawing paper*.

Place another paper on top. Holding the bottom paper stationary, press your hand firmly on top and rotate the top paper once. Remove gently.

Mount both papers on a *larger piece of colored paper*.

Shake it up, Baby!

1. Put *powdered tempera* in a *large-hole salt shaker*. Provide a variety of colors.

2. Cover *butcher paper* with a thin layer of *starch*.

3. Select a shaker. Turn it upside down, shake gently over the paper. Use a fingertip to make a few "tracks" in the paint/starch mixture. Repeat with another shaker.

Try-it With Tempera

Kitchen Cupboard Painting

Your kitchen cupboards provide a wealth of tools for interesting and easy projects. Dip, print, brush and swirl! Use objects alone or in combinations. They'll all produce wonderful works of art!

Try:

- ✖ spatula swirls
- ✖ basting brush strokes
- ✖ pizza cutter tracks
- ✖ pasta fork trails
- ✖ chopstick trails
- ✖ strainer spatters
- ✖ egg slicer prints
- ✖ baster blows
- ✖ slotted spoon stencils
- ✖ egg beater prints
- ✖ funnel trails
- ✖ wooden spoon whacks

CRazy canvases

— Artistic Fact —

Tempera is a painting medium that uses the yolks and whites of eggs, water and dry powder pigments.

Tempera paint was perfected during the Middle Ages. Artists the world over have applied this medium to all kinds of canvases and objects.

Paper does not have to be the only canvas used by students in the classroom.

Wonderful "masterpieces" can be created with little planning if you keep some of these materials around for instant canvases.

Experiment with different backgrounds for tempera paintings. Keep portfolios of all the samples. Share them at Open House.

— Here are some ideas for not-so-ordinary canvases: —

burlap	cheesecloth (prestarched)
wallpaper samples	window screens
napkins	paper towels
paper plates	sandpaper
paper bags	shingles
blocks of wood	masonite
tiles	waxed paper
aluminum foil	newspaper
corrugated cardboard	bark
giftwrap	contact paper
felt	file folders

Fingertip Frolics

Loads of art fun is at your fingertips with these easy projects.

Easy Designs

Mix flour and water to a medium consistency. Add paint to achieve desired color.

With flat hands, spread a layer of the mixture on paper. Use one fingertip to create designs.

When the mixture dries it will have a dimensional effect that you'll love to touch again!

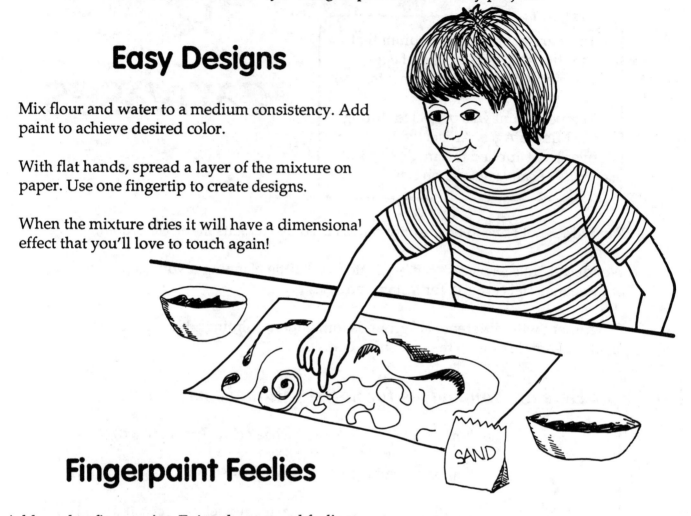

Fingerpaint Feelies

Add sand to fingerpaint. Enjoy the unusual feeling while you create the design or picture of your choice.

Macaroni Madness

Glue different shaped macaroni and noodles to cardboard. then paint the macaroni with your fingers only—NO BRUSHES.

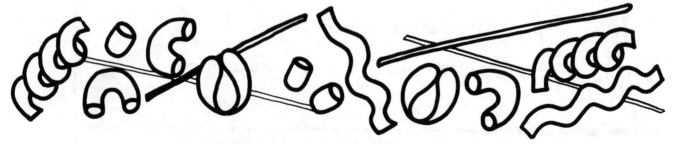

Fingertip Squares

Fold lightweight paper into four or more sections.

Use your finger to make a different design with tempera paint in each square—polka dots, stripes, squiggles, swirls, etc.

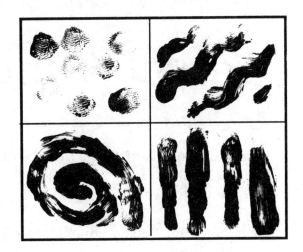

Finger Bugs

— Art Start —

Talk about the unique fingertip pattern that each person has. Examine your fingers. Do you see the pattern? Make stamp pad fingertip prints and compare prints with classmates'.

Now turn your print into an imaginary bug.

Dip your finger into paint and add feelers, legs, wings, eyes, antlers etc.

— Display —

Surround the words "Brimming With Bugs" with the imaginary bug creations.

Pretty Pussy Willows

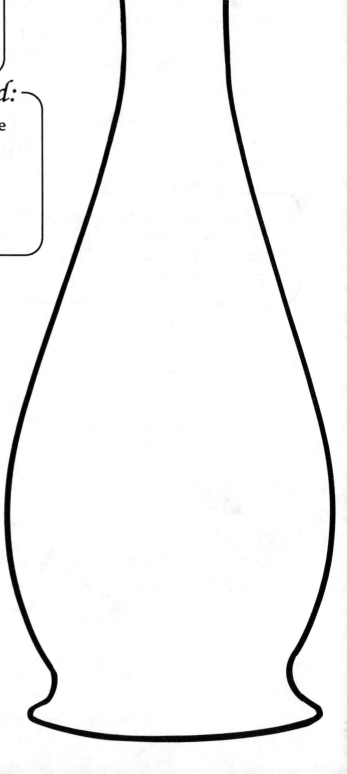

Things you'll need:

- vase pattern, reproduced on white drawing paper.
- crayons
- white tempera paint
- scissors • glue
- construction paper for mounting

Directions:

1. Color and cut out the vase.
2. Glue the vase to the construction paper backing.
3. Draw six to eight crayon branches.
4. Dip the index finger in white tempera paint and press over the stems to create pussy willow blossoms.

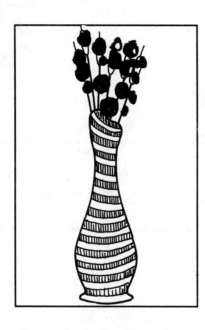

Sandy **Pictures**

Directions:

1. Mix the sand with powdered tempera in the plastic containers until the desired color is achieved.
2. Sketch a picture or design on the tagboard.
3. Brush the glue evenly over the entire surface of the tagboard.
4. Cover the glue with sand. Choose colors to accent the sketch. Shake off the excess sand.

Pulling Strings

Things you'll need:

- two colors diluted tempera paint
- large piece white construction paper
- two separate lengths of string

Directions:

1. Fold the white construction paper in half lengthwise.

2. Dip a string in one color of tempera paint. Remove the excess paint between your thumb and index finger.

3. Lay the string in a wavy pattern on one side of the paper.

4. Fold the paper over the string and set a book on top. Carefully pull out the string.

5. Open the paper and allow to dry before repeating with the second color paint and length of string.

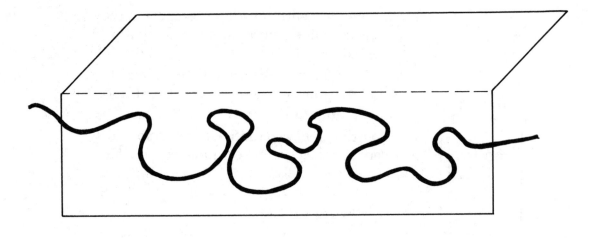

Things you'll need:

- brown tempera paint
- variety of giftwrap scraps (color selection depends on the season tree is created)
- white construction paper
- drinking straw • scissors • glue

Directions:

1. Put two to three   dots of tempera paint in the middle of white paper.
2. Carefully blow the tempera through the straw to create a tree trunk and branches.
3. Let paint dry.
4. Cut leaves, blossoms, needles from colorful wrapping paper and glue onto painted branches.

Variations:

Try using Christmas wrap for the leaves.
Use pastel paper to create spring blossoms.
Use orange and brown for fall.

Colors Everywhere

Art Start

Colors surround us everywhere. Spend some time observing the colors around you—discuss tone, shade, bright, dull, warm, hot and cool colors.

Bring a color wheel to class to share. Collect paint chips and arrange them in different harmonizing and contrasting color combinations.

Primary Only

Paint, color or use paper and glue to create a picture or design using only primary colors— RED, YELLOW and BLUE.

Mix It Up

Provide containers of the primary colors plus black and white.

Let the kids mix and create their own colors then make an original painting with their colors.

Followup Fun

Think of names for some of the colors that were created. Use your imagination, for example, "Sunburst" for a mixture of yellow and orange or "Luscious Lilac" for purple, white and pink combined.

WARM and COOL

Think of the sayings, "Red hot," or "In a blue mood."

Colors associated with *warm* are red, orange, yellow and similar shades.

Colors associated with *cool* are blue, magenta, purple and similar shades.

These projects are lessons in warm and cool colors.

Panels

Things you'll need:

- crayons: blue, green, purple (cool colors)
  red, yellow, orange (warm colors)
- 6" x 9" white construction paper

Directions:

1. Accordion-pleat the white construction paper into a fan. Open and lay flat.

2. Heavily color alternate sections of the fan with warm and cool colors. The colors can be solids, blends, designs or patterns.

W A R M	C O O L	W A R M	C O O L	W A R M	C O O L	W A R M	C O O L	W A R M

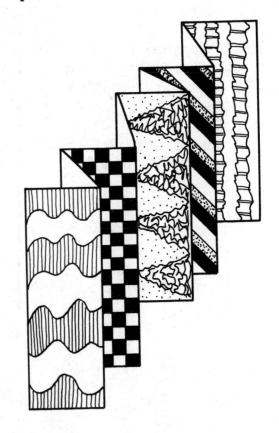

3. When finished stand the fan on a desk. When you look from one side you will see cool colors. From the other side you will see warm colors.

WARM and COOL

Line Drawing

Directions:

1. Draw a horizontal line across the paper. Draw another line, beginning at the lower left hand corner and intersecting the first line at a point about halfway.

2. Color section one and three with cool shades, section two with warm shades.

3. Use short, back-and-forth strokes and vary the colors within each section.

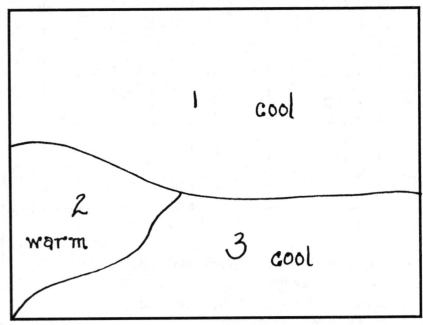

Squares

WARM and COOL

Things You'll Need:
- graph paper (large squares)
- warm, cool crayons
- pencil

Directions:

1. Sketch a simple shape on graph paper.

2. Color each square outside the shape in a different warm shade.

3. Color each square inside the shape in a different cool shade.

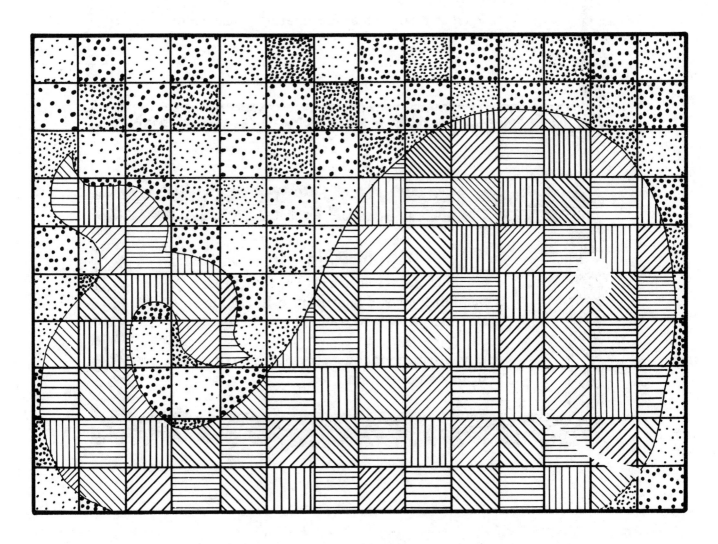

WARM and COOL

Canvas Creations

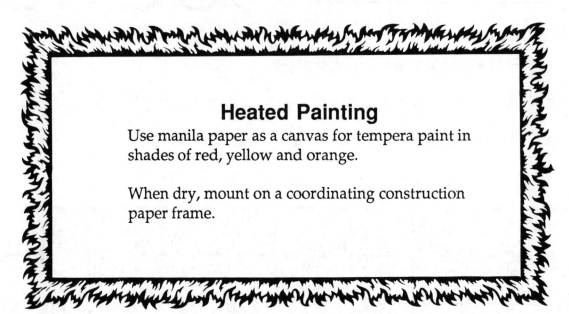

Heated Painting

Use manila paper as a canvas for tempera paint in shades of red, yellow and orange.

When dry, mount on a coordinating construction paper frame.

Chilly Painting

Use aluminum foil as a canvas for tempera paint in shades of blue, purple, light blue, lavendar, white, gray and black.

When dry, mount on a coordinating construction paper frame.

Art in an Instant

Keep a table stocked with art supplies for quick and easy projects that turn spare classroom moments into creative ones.

The activities that follow require no preparation and children can do them over and over with a different result each time—all successful.

Make a sample of each project to post at the table. You may want to briefly give directions ahead of time for younger students.

Or, if you prefer, use the ideas for large group art on days when you need an activity but don't have time for planning and preparation.

Here are the items you need to assemble for *Art in an Instant* activities:

- newspaper
- glue
- crayons
- lightweight drawing paper
- markers
- scissors
- construction paper—scraps *and* larger pieces for mounting.

The materials for each project appear in **bold-faced type** in the directions. You may cut apart and mount the directions at the art table for older students to read and follow.

SQUIGGLES

- Draw one continuous squiggle line with **black crayon**.

- Use **crayons or markers** to color each section a different color and/or design.

SIMPLY SQUARES

- Reproduce the following **grid**.

- Use **crayons or markers** to color a different picture or design in each square.

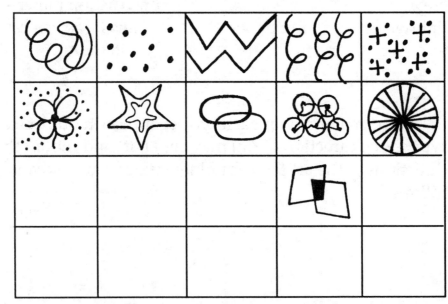

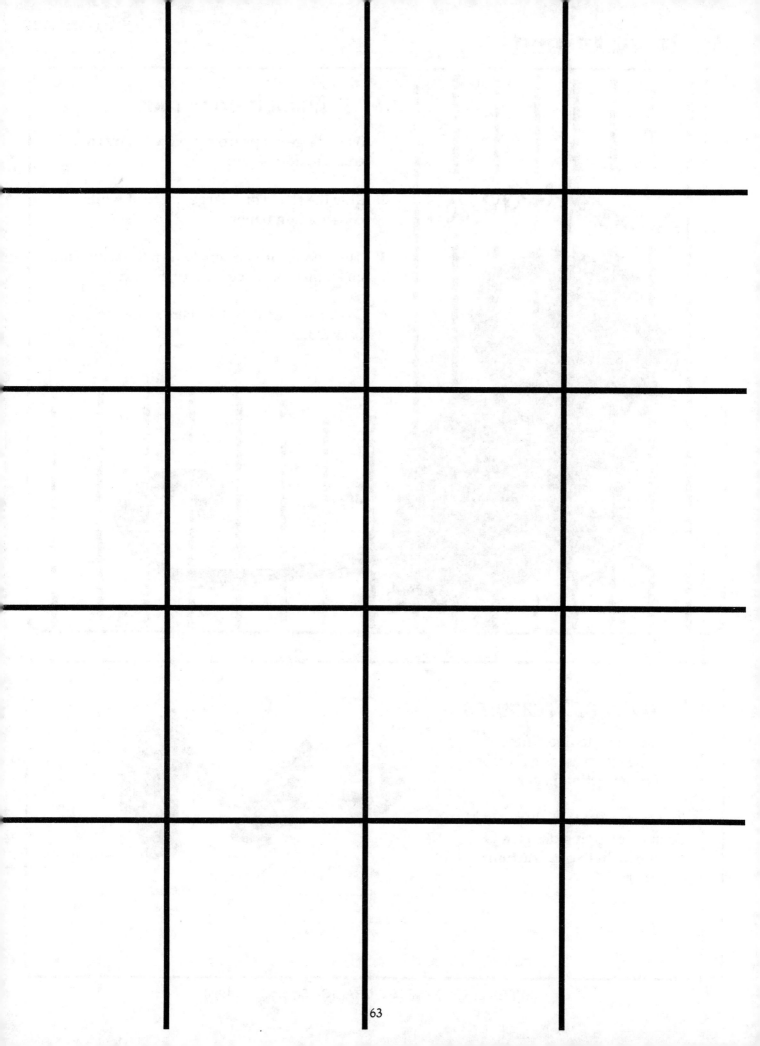

Art in an Instant

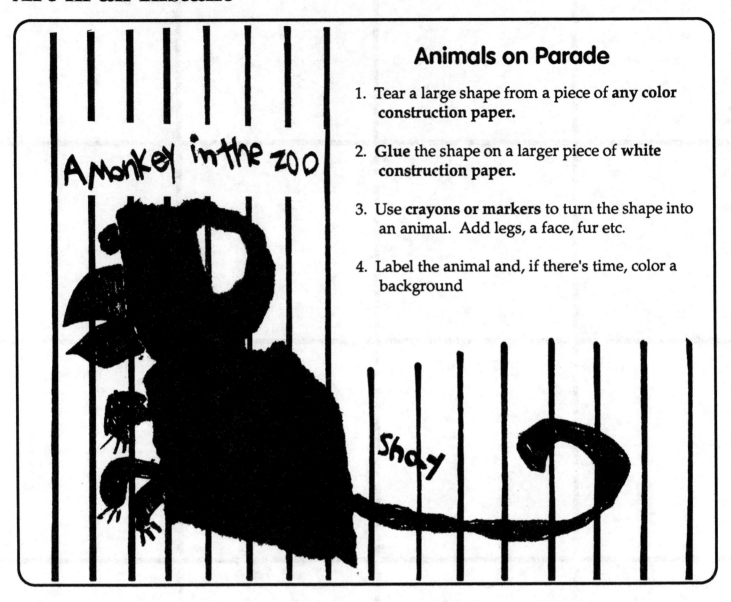

A Monkey in the zoo

Shay

Animals on Parade

1. Tear a large shape from a piece of **any color construction paper.**

2. **Glue** the shape on a larger piece of **white construction paper.**

3. Use **crayons or markers** to turn the shape into an animal. Add legs, a face, fur etc.

4. Label the animal and, if there's time, color a background

Torn Paper Treasures

1. Tear three to five different shapes from assorted scraps of **construction paper.**

2. Arrange the torn shapes in an overlapping design and **glue** them to **construction paper.**

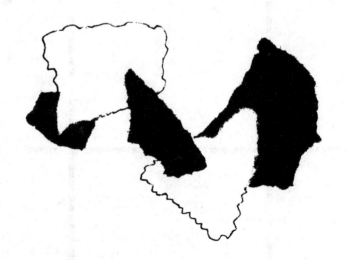

Newsprint Columns

1. Cut out a section of classified ads from the **newspaper**.
2. **Color** each ad with a different color and design.
3. Mount on **construction paper**.

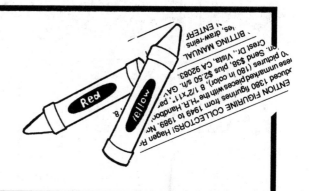

Newspaper Canvas

1. Use **markers** to outline several objects on **newspaper**.

2. With **scissors** cut around the outline and **glue** the objects on **construction paper** to create a picture.

3. Add simple details using **black marker** or **black paper cutouts**.

City Silhouettes

Cut out different length rectangles of **construction paper** and **glue** them side-by-side to a **sheet of newspaper**.

The result will resemble a silhouetted city skyline.

CLASSIFIED ART

Directions:

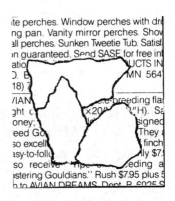

1. Starch overlapping pieces of tissue over newspaper.
2. Fold black construction paper in half lengthwise. Tear the center out to make a frame.

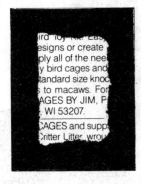

3. Press black frame on wet starch over newspaper.
4. Use the leftover center of the black paper to cut three symmetrical figures or shapes (fold paper first).
5. Press the cutouts into the starch over the frame opening.

Variations:

- Black shapes can be related to holiday
- Tissue paper colors can be changed

Things you'll need:

- dark colored construction paper (*see variations below*)
- waxed paper—same size as black construction paper
- dull pencil (or other blunt-pointed tool that won't tear the waxed paper.)
- rubber cement or stapler

Directions:

1. Use the dull pencil to carefully draw a picture, scene, or design on the "waxy" side of the waxed paper.
2. Use rubber cement to mount each corner of the waxed paper to dark construction paper.

Waxed Paper Etchings

Variations:

 Halloween ghosts on black paper

 Winter snowman or snowflakes on dark blue paper

 Summer suns on orange paper

 St. Patrick's shamrocks on forest green paper

 Thanksgiving turkeys on brown paper

CHALK TALK

Things you'll need:

- 9" x 12" white construction paper
- glue • hairspray
- pencil • colored chalk
- choice of spring patterns from following page or pattern of your own design

Directions:

1. Lightly sketch a simple spring flower or other pattern. Add some clouds, the sun, and grass.

2. Outline your sketch with glue. Let it dry.

3. Color your picture with colored chalk.

4. Spray completed pictures with hairspray to fix colored chalk in place.

Display:

These look beautiful mounted on spring colored construction paper and displayed on a bulletin board.

Variations:

Sketch *hearts* for **Valentine's Day**, *stockings* for **Christmas** or *leaves* for **Fall**.

SUPER BOOK OF ARTS & CRAFTS • *Edupress* • ©1990

69

Template Designs

Things You'll Need:

- assorted colors tempera paint
  (select paint according to season or holiday.)
- white construction paper
- colored chalk
- sponge pieces
- tagboard template

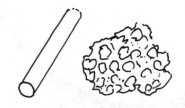

Directions:

1. Sponge paint a background using tempera on the white paper.

2. While the paint is drying, make a template by tracing a pattern of your choice on tagboard and cutting around the outline.

3. When the paint is dry, place the template on the background paper. (see Technique Tips above.) Color around the template's edge with chalk, stroking in an outward motion. The strokes should carry over to the background painting. When the template is removed, the chalk outline should remain. Move the template to a different position and repeat the steps. Make two to three template rubbings, depending on the size of the template and the background paper.

CHALK 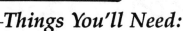 & Swirls

Things You'll Need:

- white tempera paint
- white construction paper
- starch
- colored chalk
- cardboard
- scissors

Art Start

Older students can make their own cardboard combs for this project.

Provide a rectangle of cardboard and scissors. Cut out small sections (teeth) along the edge of one length.

Directions:

1. Draw designs on the white paper with colored chalk. Cover the entire paper and fill in the designs solidly.

2. Mix paint with equal parts starch. Spread a thin layer of white paint over the entire chalk-covered paper. Use the palm of the hand to spread the paint.

3. Use a fingertip, q-tip or cardboard comb to create swirled lines in the white paint. The chalk should show through the paint.

When dry, the picture will have interesting dimension.

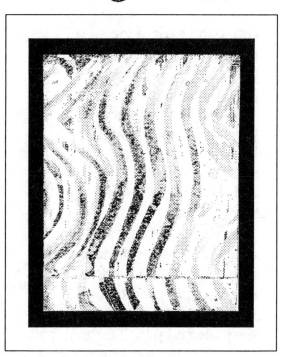

Yarn Thing

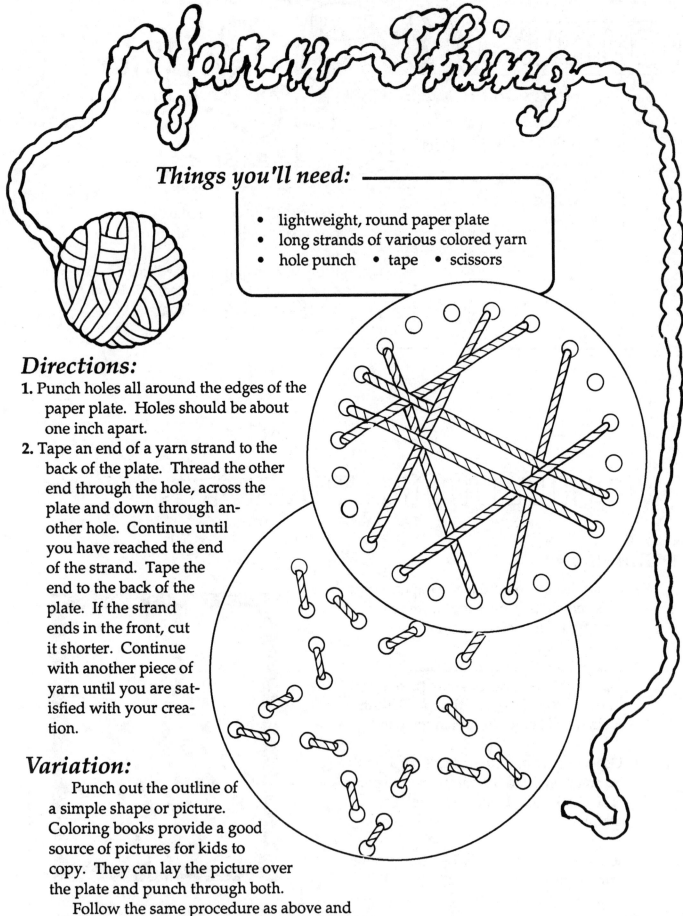

Things you'll need:

- lightweight, round paper plate
- long strands of various colored yarn
- hole punch • tape • scissors

Directions:

1. Punch holes all around the edges of the paper plate. Holes should be about one inch apart.

2. Tape an end of a yarn strand to the back of the plate. Thread the other end through the hole, across the plate and down through another hole. Continue until you have reached the end of the strand. Tape the end to the back of the plate. If the strand ends in the front, cut it shorter. Continue with another piece of yarn until you are satisfied with your creation.

Variation:

Punch out the outline of a simple shape or picture. Coloring books provide a good source of pictures for kids to copy. They can lay the picture over the plate and punch through both.

Follow the same procedure as above and stitch in and out through the holes to complete the picture.

Yarn Magic

Things You'll Need:

- cardboard shape (cut your own or use a pattern)
- glue thinned with water
- yarn—various colors

Directions:

1. Paint a small section of the cardboard shape with glue. Press yarn pieces firmly onto the cardboard, until it is completely covered. Create designs, patterns, and rows with the yarn.

2. Create dimension by gluing yarn on top of yarn.

Something New With
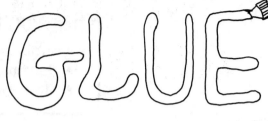

GLUE

Provide kids with glue, paper and a unique variety of items and watch the creativity begin!

Buttons and Bows

Make a festive collage using:
- ready-made bows
- buttons, assorted sizes and shapes
- curling ribbon
- giftwrap cord
- yarn

Mix and match colors or make a monochrome (one color) collage.

Puffy Stuff

Create a collage with dimension and texture using:
- fiberfill
- cotton
- quilted material scraps
- styrofoam packing pieces

Tinsel Treasures

Make a shimmering, glimmering collage using:
- tinsel
- foil
- silver glitter

See-through GLUE

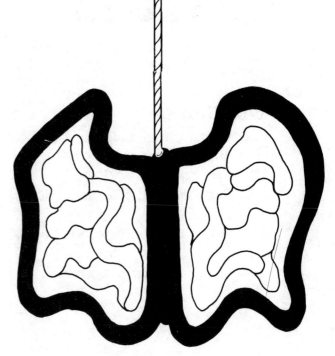

Things You'll Need:

- white glue
- food coloring
- plastic wrap
- construction paper
- scissors
- stapler
- paintbrush

Directions:

1. Mix food coloring with glue to create a variety of colors.

2. Tear off two sheets of plastic wrap, any size.

3. Use the glue mixture to paint a picture on one sheet of the plastic wrap.

4. Lay the second sheet over and press together gently with flattened hands.

5. Cut two "frames" from construction paper. (Cut them at the same time so they match exactly.) Place the plastic wrap painting between the frames and staple the frames together.

6. Trim off the excess plastic wrap.

7. Tie yarn through a hole at the top and hang in a window.

SNIFFY FRUIT

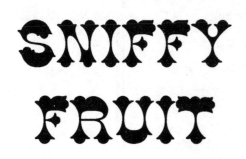

Things You'll Need:
- magazines
- scissors
- paste
- construction paper
- food extracts
- crayon

Directions:

1. Look through magazines and cut out pictures of fruit. Cut out only those in full color.

2. Paste the fruit on construction paper.

3. Add a drop of corresponding food extract.

4. Outline each fruit with dark crayon.

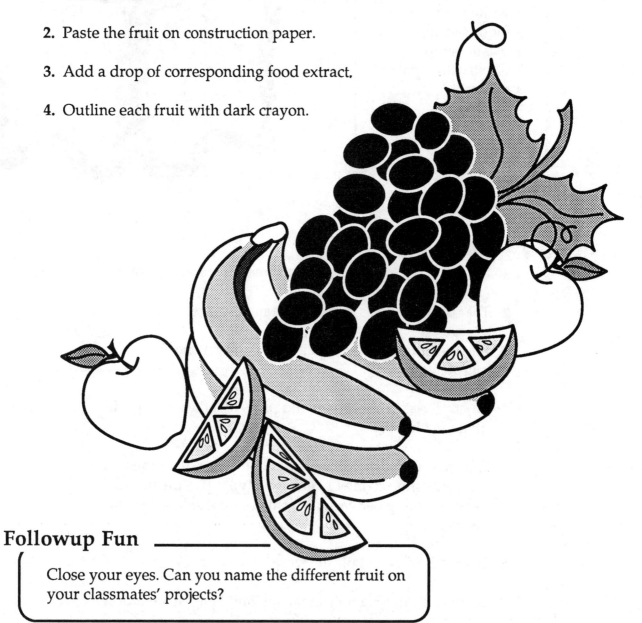

Followup Fun

Close your eyes. Can you name the different fruit on your classmates' projects?

EXPANDED ART

Things you'll need:

- 2 large, simple pictures of the same size from a magazine, preferably without writing
- One 9" x 12" manila construction paper
- ruler • scissors • pencil

Directions:

1. Turn both magazine pictures to the back side and measure 1" strips. Letter the strips **A, B, C, . . .** on both pictures going from **right** to **left**.

backside picture 1

G F E D C B A

G F E D C B A

backside picture 2

2. Cut out strips.

3. Glue strips onto the 9" x 12" piece of construction paper starting at the left with strip A from picture 1, then strip A from picture 2, continuing on with both strip Bs, Cs, etc.

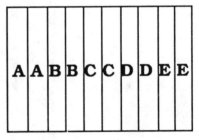

front of picture

A A B B C C D D E E

4. You will end up with 2 expanded pictures.

5. If the expanded picture does not cover the background paper, trim to fit.

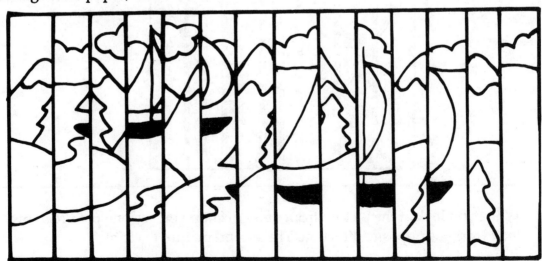

SUPER BOOK OF ARTS & CRAFTS • *Edupress* • ©1990

77

Two-Sided Pictures

Things You'll Need:

- 9"x12" (half sheet) white construction paper
- two 9'x12" magazine pictures
- ruler • pencil
- paste • scissors

Directions:

1. Use a ruler to measure 1"(2.5 cm) strips on each magazine picture. cut the strips apart. KEEP THEM IN ORDER!

2. Fold each strip in half lengthwise.

3. Working left to right, begin with the first strip from one picture. Paste the left side down on the left edge of the construction paper. The right half of the strip should be folded out, away from the paper. Now paste the left half of the first strip from the second picture to the right half of the first strip. The right half can now be pasted to the paper, butting up against the fold. Continue with this procedure until all strips are used. Trim edges.

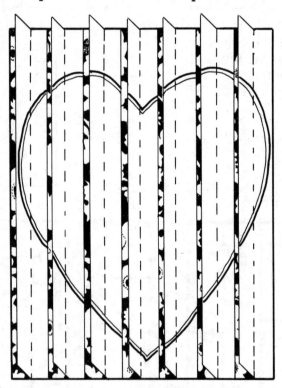

When you look at the picture from one direction you see one picture. Now look from the opposite direction. The second picture is visible.

Crepe Paper Creations

Streamer Fun

- Ask your local paint store for **paint stirrers**.

- Cut several different-colored strips of **crepe paper**, varying in length.

- **Glue** the streamers to the end of the paint stirrer.

- Head outside for some streamer fun, or stay indoors and move the streamers to music.

The Wave

- Start with a strip of **construction paper**.

- **Glue** short strips of **crepe paper** on the ends, only, to the paper.

- Wind them in and out for a "stand up" wave effect.

Say Cheese!

Here's a cute project that takes on its own tasty dimension!

Things You'll Need:
- brown construction paper
- construction paper (any color) for background
- sponge triangle
- scissors   • glue
- assorted construction paper scraps

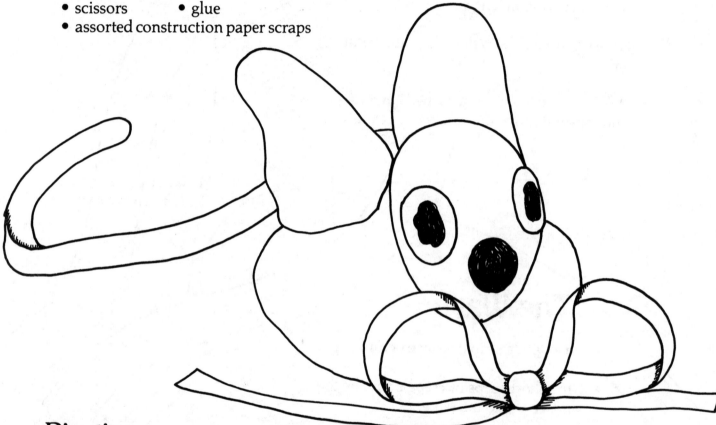

Directions:

1. Cut an oval mouse body and two half-circle ears. Fold the ears in half. Glue them to the background paper as shown. (Only half the ear will be glued. The other half should stick out from the paper.)

2. Curl a strip of paper around a pencil and glue for a tail.

3. Glue the triangular sponge next to the mouse. Say Cheese, Please!

Paper Plate Put-Togethers

Things You'll Need:

- dinner size, lightweight paper plates, white
- paint   • paintbrush
- glue • scissors
- construction paper—varied colors for mounting

Directions:

1. Cut the center out of a paper plate. (Save the center for another project.)

2. Cut the scalloped edge into 4 sections, approximately the same length.

3. Paint the rounded side of each section the colors of your choice.

4. When dry, spread glue on each end of the unpainted sides and arrange them in a random design on colored construction paper.

Technique Tips

In order to achieve a dimensional effect put glue only on the ends of the plate sections. Paint is more effective than coloring as crayon pressure will flatten the plates.

TISSUE PAPER TRICKS

Start with a Background

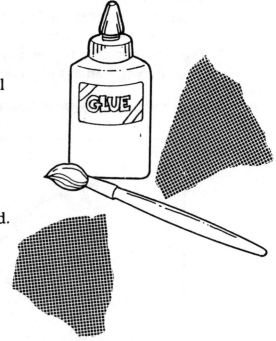

Turn any size white construction paper into a colorful canvas by painting on overlapping strips, squares or torn tissue shapes. Completely cover the background paper.

Then try one of these easy finishing touches:

• Glue a magazine cut out over the tissue background.

• Glue construction paper shapes or pictures.

• Create a picture using colorful marking pens.

Variation

Glue tissue pieces to a permanent background on a slick surface like a plastic foam meat tray or aluminum pie pan. Peel translucent shape from tray or pan when dry. Trim if necessary and add pipe cleaner (butterfly) or other detail.

TISSUE PAPER TRICKS

Mountain Scenes

Things You'll Need:

- 1/4 sheet white construction paper
- blue, pink, yellow, green and gray tissue paper
- starch • paintbrush

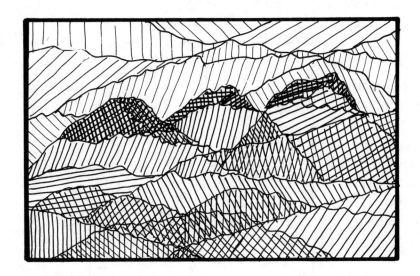

Directions:

1. Work from the bottom of the paper to the top.

2. Tear narrow strips of tissue. Lay them across the construction paper and brush down with starch.

3. Begin with green tissue. Next tear mountains out of gray paper.

4. Then create a sky using blue, pink, and yellow tissue. Overlap colors to create shapes and shadows. Paper space does not have to be completely covered.

5. Trim around the edges.

Circled Tissue

- Begin with a colorful square of construction paper.

- Cut a white circle to fit in the square and glue in place.

- Tear tissue paper strips slightly larger than the diameter of the circle. Arrange the strips in a circular pattern over the white circle and "paint" into place using starch or diluted white glue.

- Add a variety of torn tissue shapes in the very center.

- Drops of full strength glue will add texture and dimension.

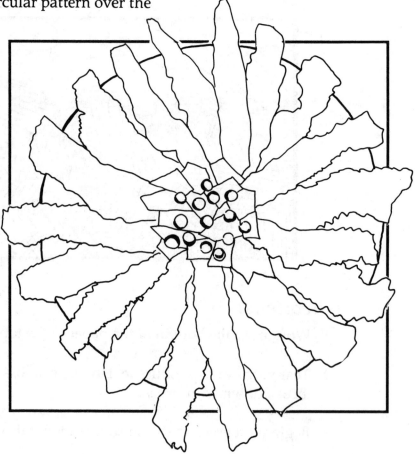

TISSUE PAPER TRICKS

Silhouettes in the Sunset

⌐ Things You'll Need: ¬

- 12"x18" white construction paper
- tissue paper: yellow, orange, red & brown (approximately 3-4 inches wide and 18" long)
- 12"x18" black construction paper
- starch • paintbrush
- glue • scissors • white chalk

Directions:

1. Starch tissue paper on white construction paper in the order illustrated leaving spaces of white in between.

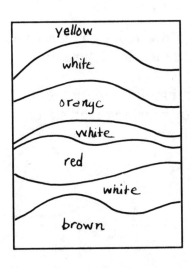

2. On the black construction paper use chalk to draw a frame around the edge and the silhouette of a tree inside.

3. Cut out on chalk lines being careful not to cut through the frame.

4. Glue, chalk side down, over the tissue design.

A sunset will show through the black silhouetted tree.

TISSUE PAPER TRICKS

Bleached Pictures

Things You'll Need:

- bleach • water
- mixing containers
- cotton swabs • scissors
- two tissue paper squares, any size and color
- starch • paintbrush
- construction paper

Caution children regarding bleach. Even though the mixture is highly diluted, safety should still be discussed.

Directions:

1. Mix one part bleach with 10 parts water.

2. Cut two identical squares of contrasting color tissue paper.

3. Using a cotton swab, draw a design on each tissue square with the bleach mixture.

4. Overlap the tissue and mount the squares to construction paper by brushing with starch.

5. Trim around the edges.

Easy Designs

Here are some quick and easy variations using tissue shapes.

Have on hand:
- variety of colored tissue paper
- scissors • crayons
- paintbrush • starch
- colored markers • construction paper

1 Cut tissue shapes. Arrange shapes on white construction paper. Paint with starch. When dry, outline each shape with colored marker.

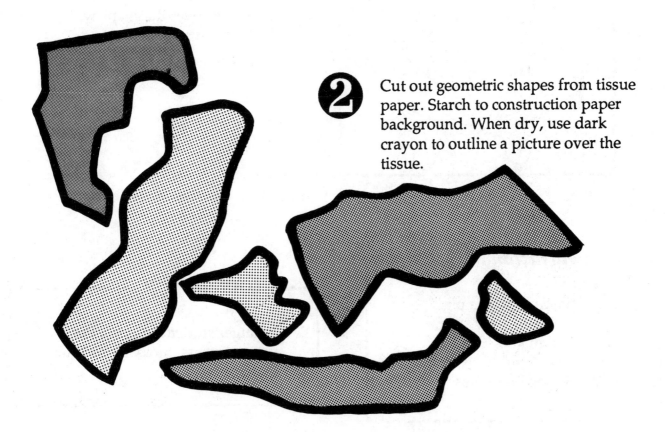

2 Cut out geometric shapes from tissue paper. Starch to construction paper background. When dry, use dark crayon to outline a picture over the tissue.

TISSUE PAPER TRICKS

Crumpled Shapes

Children of any age can successfully create these tissue paper shapes.

Directions:

1. Begin with a tagboard pattern.

2. Use one of your own design, one of the quick-and-easy patterns in this book, or the chick, following, for a cute Spring creation.

3. Cut a large quantity of 2-inch (5cm) tissue squares.

4. Wrap one square of tissue over the end of a pencil. Put a dot of glue on the tip and press down onto the tagboard.

5. Completely cover the shape with the raised tissue.

Variation

 harvest cornucopia

 March kites

 Spring butterflies

Technique Tip

Younger students can roll the tissue squares into balls and glue in place.

TISSUE SHAPES

Things you'll need:
- tissue paper in assorted colors
- mixture of equal parts glue and water
- paint brush
- two sheets waxed paper
- newspaper • string

Directions:

1. Spread newspaper over the work area. Lay one sheet of waxed paper on the newspaper and "paint" it with the glue mixture.
2. Cover the waxed paper completely with torn pieces of tissue. Paint again with the glue mixture.
3. Dip string into the glue mixture and make an outline of a shape on the waxed paper. The ends of the string must meet to make a complete shape.
4. Lay the second sheet of waxed paper over the tissue and string. Press until it sticks firmly.
5. Allow to dry completely then trim around the design right next to the string.

Suggested Shapes: Valentine heart, Butterflies, Fish

Display: Hang in a window or from the ceiling.

FILIGREE

ARTISTIC FACT

Filigree is a form of ornamental artwork of a delicate or intricate design. The material used is usually fine wire of gold, silver or copper.

THINGS YOU'LL NEED:

- string
- gold, silver or bronze paint
- glue
- construction paper backing

DIRECTIONS:

1. Mix paint with glue.

2. Dip string in mixture, pull out between the thumb and index finger to remove excess.

3. Rearrange the string in an intricate pattern on the construction paper. Press into place.

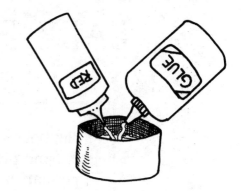

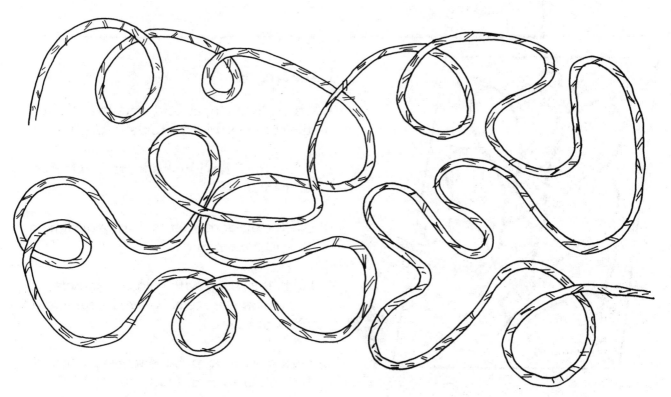

STAINED GLASS

Artistic Facts

Stained glass is colored glass that has been cut into pieces and reassembled to form a picture or design. The pieces are held together by strips of lead. The picture shines when the glass is lit. That is why stained glass is used mainly for windows.

Simulate stained glass windows.

EASY FOIL WINDOWS

Things you'll need:

- chipboard (any size)
- foil and plastic wrap (cut slightly larger than chipboard)
- permanent marking pens—black plus assorted colors
- masking tape

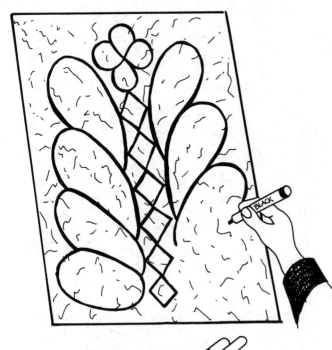

Directions:

1. Crumple foil, open and smooth out, cover the chipboard. Tape to the backside.

2. Cover the foil with plastic wrap. **Do not** tape in place.

3. Use the black marker to draw a design on the plastic wrap.

4. Fill in the panes with colored markers. Leave some space between the color and the black outlines.

5. Turn plastic wrap to the reverse side and tape securely over foil.

EASY EMBOSSING

Here are two projects that achieve an embossed effect and are suitable for several skill levels.

ARTISTIC FACTS

Embossing is a process in which a raised design is pressed on a material such as leather, paper, wood or metal.

True embossing has a pressed background leaving the design in relief. Repousse is a form of embossing in which the raised design is created from the back.

"ANTIQUED" EMBOSSING

THINGS YOU'LL NEED:

- tagboard or chipboard, any shape or size
- india ink, shoepolish or marking pens
- glue • aluminum foil
- paint brush

DIRECTIONS:

1. Make a design on tagboard with a thick stream of glue. Keep the lines of glue a good distance apart. Dry overnight or until glue has hardened.
2. Make a mixture of equal parts water and glue. Paint over the entire surface of the tagboard.
3. Tear a piece of foil large enough to cover the tagboard plus overlap behind. Crumple the foil lightly, uncrumple and press over the glued surface. Begin in the center and work out.
4. Paint the embossed foil with ink or shoepolish. Wipe gently to highlight the raised areas. If marking pens are used, color only the unraised sections.

EMBOSSED BEANS

THINGS YOU'LL NEED:

- tagboard or chipboard
- variety of beans
- glue • aluminum foil

DIRECTIONS:

1. Glue the beans to the tagboard in a random design. Allow the glue to set.
2. Carefully press and mold the foil over the bean design. Fold the extra foil over the back and secure.

Sculpture

Followup Fun

Make a list of famous monuments and sculptures.

Carve a soap sculpture at home. Use a plastic knife or craft stick.

Foil Sculpture

Start with a large sheet of aluminum foil.

Twist, shape, bend and crumple the foil into an interesting shape.

Use a craft stick to display this work of art. Poke one end of the stick into the sculpture. Poke the other end into a ball of clay.

Painted Sculptures

Things You'll Need:

- tempera paints
- brushes
- thin cardboard

Directions:

1. Cut cardboard into a variety of shapes. Cut an uneven number.

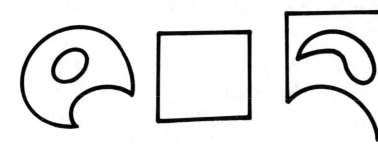

Openings can be cut in some of the shapes.

2. Paint the pieces of cardboard with tempera. You can use all primary colors, cool colors, warm—whatever you choose! Let pieces dry.

3. Cut a slot in one piece of cardboard. Insert the edge of another piece into the slot.

4. Continue cutting slots until all pieces are attached. The sculpture should be freestanding.

Diorama Dazzlers

Artistic Fact

A **diorama** is an exhibit showing modeled figures in front of a painted or modeled background. The models become smaller toward the back of the scene. Diorama comes from the Greek words meaning "a view through." They can be lifesize or miniature models.

Museums use dioramas to show historical events, plants and animals in natural settings.

Art Start

Brainstorm a list of good settings for a diorama. Here are some suggestions:

- prehistoric days
- dinosaurs
- Alaskan Eskimos
- animals in the jungle
- desert life
- Antarctic penguins
- Revolutionary War
- Indian life
- barnyard
- underwater

Easy Diorama

Directions:

1. Create a **construction paper** scene on a **paper plate**. Cut out the center section of a second plate.
2. Staple the plates together, curved sides out.

NOTE: Older students can create a more artistically-correct diorama by raising some of their cutouts off the plate with sponge pieces or accordion-folded paper.

Boxed Diorama

A shoebox makes a great setting for a diorama.

Take the lid off. Turn the box on its side. Paint the box. (You may need to add some liquid soap to the paint.)

Create a scene inside the box. Paint the background first. Bring models from home, cut out magazine pictures or create and color your own shapes and figures.

Remember to make the figures in the front larger than the figures in the back.

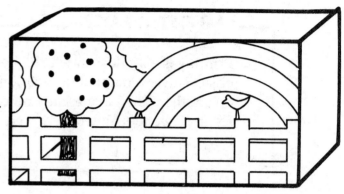

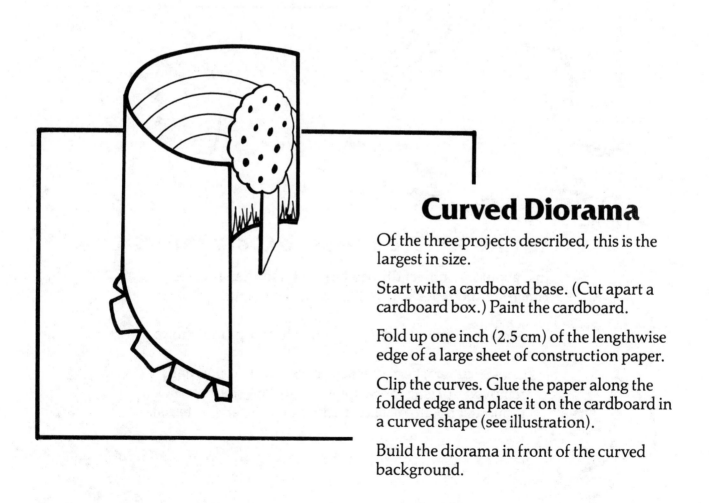

Curved Diorama

Of the three projects described, this is the largest in size.

Start with a cardboard base. (Cut apart a cardboard box.) Paint the cardboard.

Fold up one inch (2.5 cm) of the lengthwise edge of a large sheet of construction paper.

Clip the curves. Glue the paper along the folded edge and place it on the cardboard in a curved shape (see illustration).

Build the diorama in front of the curved background.

FUN WITH PRINTING

Printing can be rewarding at any age. Choose the method best suited to your students.

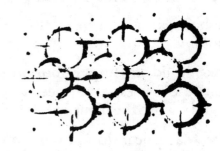

ARTISTIC FACT

Printing is a method in which one object leaves a painted impression on another. The Japanese are noted for their wonderful wood-carved ink prints.

TECHNIQUE TIPS

Create a stamp pad by setting a sponge in a shallow pan and covering it with tempera paint. Use a separate pan for each color.

PRINTING FOR BEGINNERS—GADGET PRINTS

Just about **any object** dipped in **paint** and then pressed to **construction paper** will yield rewarding results.

Try some of these "gadgets" for your first printing efforts:

Cookie cutters, berry baskets, cans (cleaned and ends removed), plastic forks, sponges cut into shap es, old-fashioned potato masher, natural objects (sticks, ferns).

Can-can Prints

Things you'll need:

- can—any size, cleaned and dried
- yarn or string
- sponge • shallow pan
- tempera paint
- white construction paper

Directions:

1. Use glue to make a simple line design around a can.

2. Press yarn firmly to the glue.

3. Place the sponge in a shallow pan and cover it with paint. This will act as a stamp pad.

4. Roll the can over the "stamp pad."

5. When string is coated with paint roll the can over the construction paper. Repeat many times, overlapping the rolls.

6. Additional colors can be added as each layer of paint begins to dry. Kids can share cans so paint colors don't mix.

FUN WITH PRINTING

PRINTING PLATE

Use a **plastic knife** and **toothpick** to "carve" a design in a **foam meat-packing tray**. (Cut the sides off first.)

Use a **brayer** to roll **tempera paint** over the carved picture or design.

Press the tray to **paper** to make a printed impression.

DISPLAY

Mount both the print and the carved original side by side on construction paper.

Sponge Printed Flowers

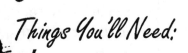

Things You'll Need:

- half-sheet white construction paper
- sponges • scissors
- tempera paint
- paper towels

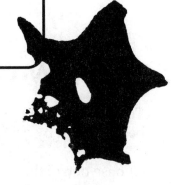

Teacher Preparation:

1. Cut sponges into various "petal" shapes.

2. Pour a variety of paint colors on paper towel pads.

Directions:

1. Select a sponge, press into paint then on the paper.

2. Repeat with several other sponge shapes and paint colors.

3. Use your fingertip to put a "dab" of paint in the center of each flower, and to add stems and leaves.

MAKE SOME MOSAICS

COLOR MOSAIC

Tear or cut small pieces from magazine pictures. Construction paper can also be used. Sort by color.

Choose one of these variations:

Paste the colors to form a shape such as a kite for March or a stocking for Christmas.

Paste the colors in stripes from warm to cool or in primary colors (red, blue, yellow).

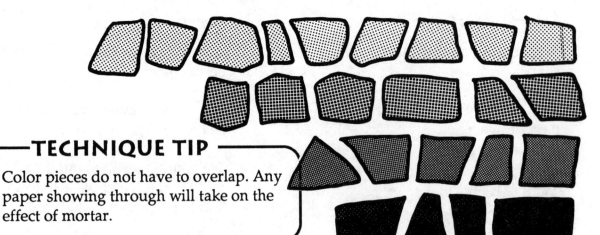

TECHNIQUE TIP

Color pieces do not have to overlap. Any paper showing through will take on the effect of mortar.

WHALE OF A MOSAIC

Work in pairs to make a super-big mosaic.

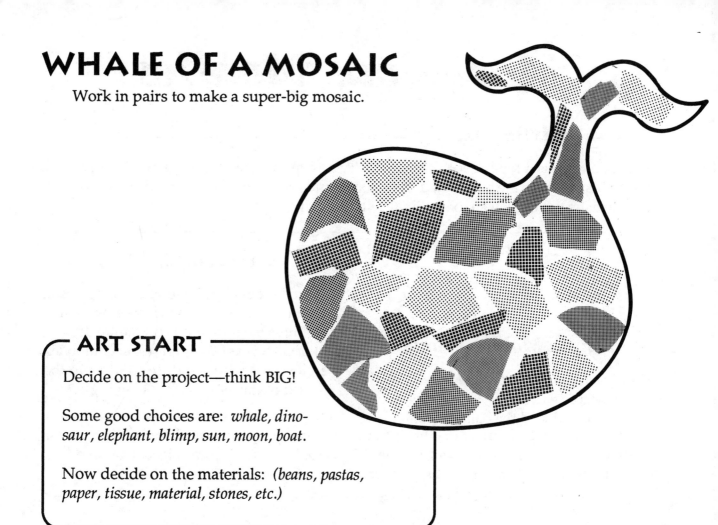

ART START

Decide on the project—think BIG!

Some good choices are: *whale, dinosaur, elephant, blimp, sun, moon, boat.*

Now decide on the materials: *(beans, pastas, paper, tissue, material, stones, etc.)*

DIRECTIONS:

1. Cut a large shape from black, grey or white butcher paper.

2. Working from opposite ends, create a mosaic using the materials you have agreed upon.

3. Background paper may show through.

4. Paint the finished project with diluted glue to prevent ends from peeling up.

TECHNIQUE TIP

This may take several days to complete. It's a good project to set aside and work on during free class time.

Marvelous Mobiles

Artistic Fact

A mobile is a type of sculpture that moves mainly through the act of air circulation. Most mobiles are suspended from above and are delicately balanced. They are artistic not only in shape but in the shadow they cast.

Technique Tip

A true mobile has several objects carefully balanced. The mobile on these two pages requires balance and is best suited for older students. Several "single object" mobiles follow that will introduce children to the world of this wonderful "hanging art."

Simple Mobile Frame

Loop each end of a curved wire. Attach an object to each loop. Tie a string to the wire and find the balance point.
Form a loop in the wire at that balance point by carefully twisting the wire with pliers. Attach one end of a second wire at the balance point. Hang a third object from the remaining looped end. Find the balance point on the second wire and hang.

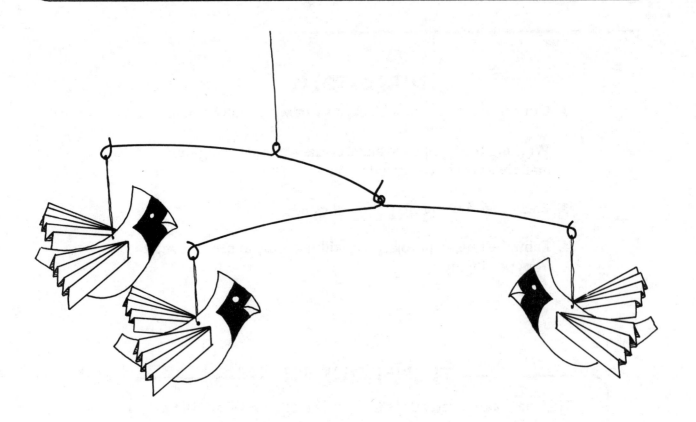

Cardinal Mobile

Things You'll Need:
- red construction paper
- red tissue paper
- black crayon • scissors

Directions:

1. Use the pattern to cut the bird from red construction paper.

2. Color both sides of the head section black, leaving a red beak and eye.

3. Fan fold the red tissue paper. Cut the bird on the dotted lines and pull the tissue wings through.

4. Punch a hole on the "X" and hang on the mobile frame.

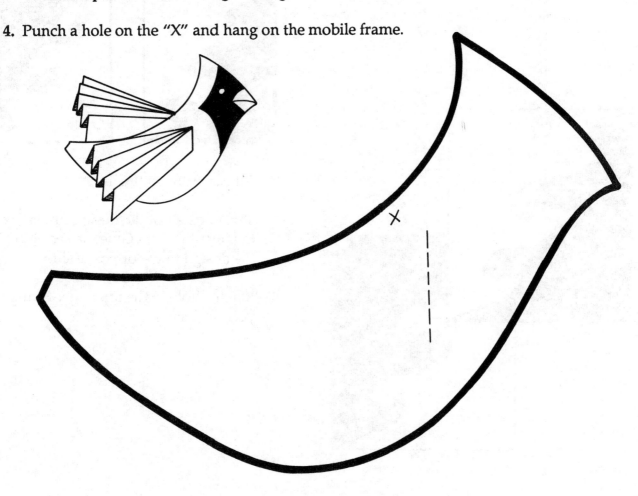

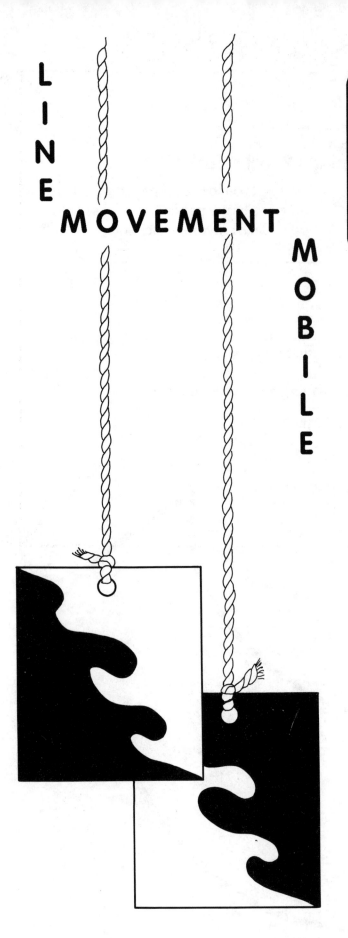

LINE MOVEMENT MOBILE

Directions:

1. Draw a "moving" line diagonally across one piece of paper very lightly with pencil.

2. Cut carefully on the line.

3. Glue one half of the design to a side of the uncut paper. Glue the second half of the design to the opposite side.

4. Punch a hole in the top edge. String with yarn and hang.

PINWHEEL HANGINGS

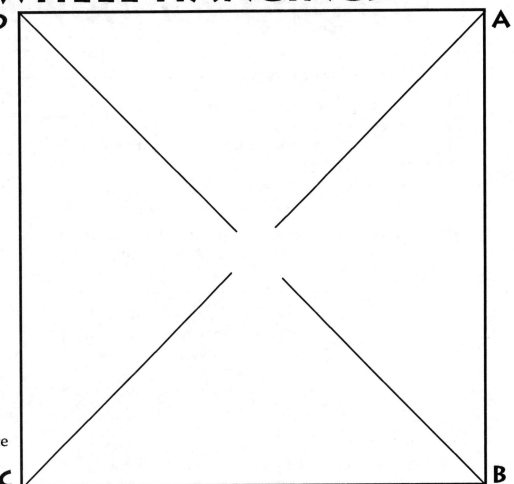

D   A

C   B

1. Reproduce pinwheel pattern on white construction paper.

2. Use crayons to decorate on one side of the square.

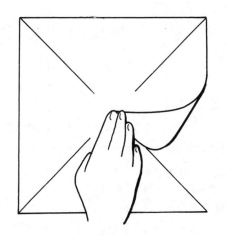

3. Cut on lines A, B, C, D.

4. Glue every other point to the center.

5. Make hole in one tip and hang with yarn.

SUPER BOOK OF ARTS & CRAFTS • *Edupress* • ©1990

Hanging Rainbow Mobile

Art Start

Talk about the shape and colors in a rainbow.

Things You'll Need:

- 18" (45cm) sheet waxed paper
- starch • paintbrush
- 2" (5cm) tissue paper squares—red, orange, green, purple
- yarn • glue
- white construction paper

Directions:

1. Lay the waxed paper flat. Glue two yarn arcs to the waxed paper to serve as top and bottom guides.

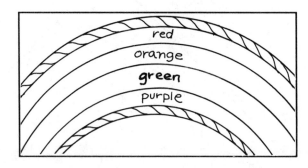

red
orange
green
purple

2. Starch arcs of overlapping tissue squares in the order shown between the yarn.

3. Let dry. Peel off the waxed paper carefully.

4. Trim tissue, if necessary. Cut white puffy clouds to glue to each end of the rainbow.

5. Hang with V-shaped yarn.

Technique Tip

- There should be no gaps in the tissue paper.

- Starch as you progress.

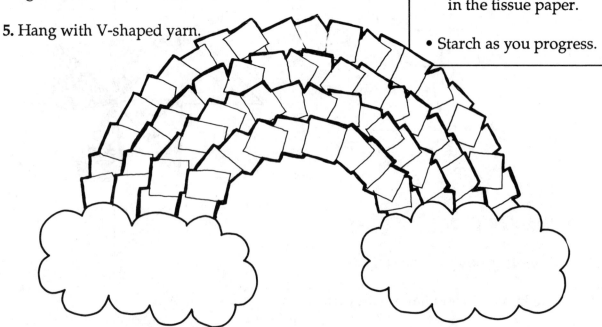

MOBILE CUTOUTS

THINGS YOU'LL NEED:
- 9" (23cm) yellow construction paper circle
- scissors   • glue   • thin yarn

DIRECTIONS:

1. Draw a design around the edge of the circle. Cut out the design.

2. Cut another circle out of the center. Then cut that circle smaller so it can swing freely in the middle of the large circle. Repeat the cut out design on the smaller circle.

3. Use yarn to hang the small circle in the middle of the larger one. Be sure the yarn is also glued to the larger shape and long enough to hang the mobile.

Try these ideas too:

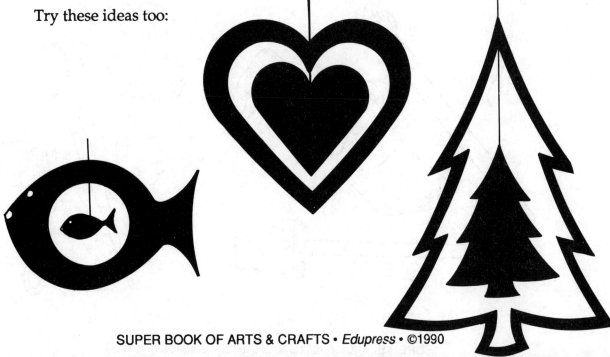

Marvelous Murals

Artistic Fact

A mural is a picture or design that decorates a large area such as a wall or ceiling. Some are painted directly on the surface, others are made of small pieces of stone, glass or other material.

Technique Tip

Murals offer a wonderful opportunity for cooperative learning. Groups can plan colors, themes and responsibilities before they begin.

Here are several different mural projects to brighten your classroom walls.

Movement Mural

Station 6-8 people around a large piece of **butcher paper**. Supply each with a different color **paint** and **various painting materials** (i.e. different width brushes, toothbrushes, sponges, etc.). Upon hearing an agreed-upon signal, the "artists" rotate around the table, carrying with them their paint color and painting implement. Make one revolution around the mural.

Classroom Quilt

Art Start

Choose a theme. This may coordinate with curriculum currently being studied, a holiday or season.

Involve students in the decision-making process.

Directions and Display

1. Individual pictures corresponding with the theme are colored or painted on a square of white drawing paper by each member of the class.

2. Assemble the pictures in quilt-fashion on the wall to create a large mural. Add a colorful border around the quilt.

Animals

Spray a Mural

Fill clean, **empty spray bottles** (from household cleaners) with diluted **tempera paint**. Start with a little **water** then continue to add until paint is thin enough to be sprayed.

Prepare a variety of cut out **cardboard shapes**. The group working on the mural can decide on the shapes.

Arrange the shapes on a mural-size sheet of **butcher paper**. Each group member sprays the mural with a different color paint. When dry, remove the shapes.

Silhouette Collage

Things You'll Need:

- 12"x18" construction paper - any color
- white butcher paper
- scissors • glure
- magazines
- overhead projector

Directions

Teacher:
1. Use the overhead projector to cast a silhouette of each student's head. Trace the silhouette on white butcher paper. the image should not be larger than the construction paper.

Student
1. Cut out the silhouette. Glue it to the large sheet of construction paper

2. Cut out pictures from magazines that show things you like—foods, interests, hobbies, sports, pets, cars.

3. Glue the pictures to the silhouette in a collage.

Real Life "ME"

Things You'll Need:

- two body lengths white butcher paper
- paint • crayons • markers
- scissors • stapler
- newspaper • yarn

Directions:

1. Children work in pairs. One lies down on the butcher paper, face up. The partner traces the body's outline.

2. Paint what you think you look like, front and back. "Dress" yourself.

3. Cut out around the outline. Staple the front to the back around the outside edge, leaving a section open.

4. Lightly stuff the shape with newspaper. Staple closed the opening.

Variation and Display

Don't paint on clothing. Bring clothes from home. Seat the bodies in the chairs for Open house night. Can parents find their child?

SELF PORTRAIT

Art Start

Before you begin, talk about physical characteristics—colors, shapes, hairstyles and so forth.

Bring some mirrors to class so that children can look while they sketch.

Things you'll need:

- 12" x 18" white construction paper
- black crayon
- watercolors • brush

Directions:

1. Sketch yourself from the shoulders up. Try to make it look just like you. Make sure you use the entire paper.

2. Outline the sketch with a black crayon.

3. Paint the entire picture with watercolors.

Display:

Mount the portraits on black construction paper and display them on the bulletin board for Back to School or Open House. Don't write student names on the front. Parents try to guess who each person is. Can they recognize their own child? Can classmates recognize each other?

EXPRESS YOURSELF

Children share personal information through art. Choose the project best suited to your students.

Things you'll need:

- magazine
- scissors
- paint brush
- glue
- crayons
- construction paper

Art Start

Take some time to talk with children about the things they like to do. Ask them to share sports activities and pasttimes.

Then talk about the things they don't like.

Brainstorm descriptive words then ask students to decide which words best describe them. Can they think of any others?

ME

Reproduce **ME** pattern (following) for each student.

Students: Outline each letter with bold, heavy crayon in your favorite colors.

Cut out magazine pictures that show things you like to do, eat, wear and so on.

Paint over the magazine pictures with diluted glue to hold down loose picture edges. Mount on colored construction paper.

This makes an excellent cover for a "ME" book.

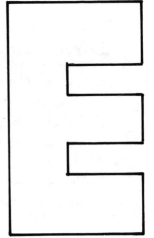

What A Pleasure!

LITTLE RUGGED! The Best

Put it in Words

Cut words and letters that describe your personality and appearance from magazines and glue them to construction paper.

If you cannot find complete words, cut apart letters and use them to spell out the descriptive words. (Keep a dictionary nearby.)

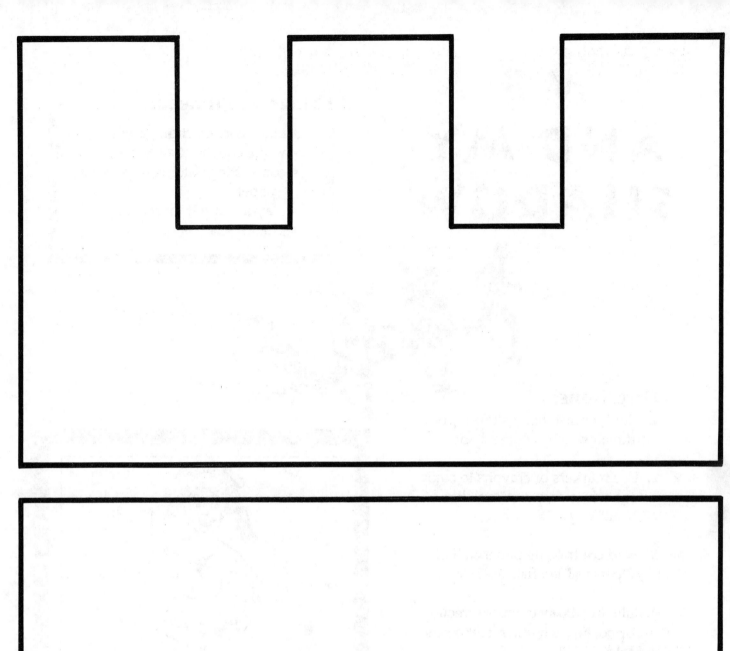

ME AND MY SHADOW

Things you'll need:

- black construction paper
- white construction paper
- contrasting color construction paper
- crayons or felt markers
- glue • scissors

Directions:

1. Cut identical body shapes from the black and white paper.

2. Use markers or crayons to color the white shape to "look like you."

3. Fold contrasting paper in half. Open and lay flat.

4. Glue the body cutouts directly opposite each other, feet on the fold.

Followup Fun:

Head outside for some *real* shadow experiences.

- Play "Shadow Tag."
- Take turns using chalk to trace a classmate's shadow on the playground.
- Can you "get rid of" your shadow?

Things you'll need:

- 9" by 12" white construction paper

- crayons, assorted colors

NAME SHADOWS

Directions

1. Fold the paper in half, lengthwise.

2. Use crayon to heavily print or write your name very large and very bold. The bottom of each letter should touch the fold.

3. Fold the paper over and gently rub from side to side. This will transfer the name to the other side of the folded line.

4. Open the paper and go over the backwards name with the same dark crayon.

5. Use various colored crayons to make lines following the contour of the letters to the outside edge of the paper.

NAME FRAME

Create a personalized frame to put around a self-portrait or other art project.

With bold crayon write your name over and over again on strips of construction paper. Glue the strips around the art project to create a frame.

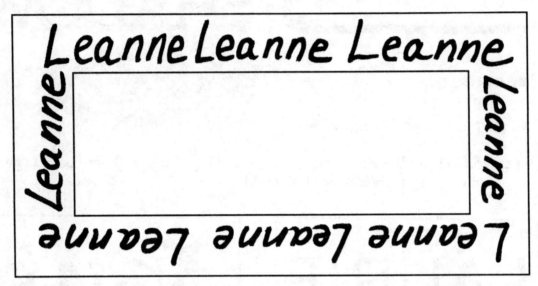

NAME FLAME

Fold a piece of 9"x12" construction paper in half lengthwise.

Write or print your name along the fold. Cut around the names and on the fold between the letters. See illustration.

Open the paper and glue to a larger piece of construction paper.

Add a flame to the top to create an un- usual name candle.

VARIATION:

✡ Create a **Hanukkah** menorah with the name flame as the center candle.

☆ Create a **Christmas** "window" by mounting the name flames to the classroom wall and adding paper strip window panes.

Initial Event

The initials of your name provide lots of quick and easy creative fun.

Initial Creatures

Draw the initials of your first and last name in big, bold crayon letters on a sheet of drawing paper.

Use your imagination and add a head, feet, wings, and other animal features of your choice.

—Followup Fun—

Write a silly story about your initial creature.

Initials Square

Fold a sheet of drawing paper into smaller squares. (The older the student the smaller the square).

Fill each square with an initial from your first, middle and last name.

Fill the first square with the initial from your first name. The next square will have your middle initial and so on until all the squares have been filled.

Vary the colors of the initials.

Fold paper into thirds. Print your first, middle and last initial in the boxes. Make them large enough to fill the space.

Color designs around each letter.

Quick & Easy Pattern Projects

Lots of Leaf Ideas

Trace the pattern on **construction paper**.

Use **fall-colored crayons** to make a patchwork design inside the leaf.

Place the leaf pattern on **black construction paper**. Rub **chalk** on the edges of the pattern.

Use a **facial tissue** to rub the chalk in an outward motion onto the black paper.

When the pattern is removed a "hazy" leaf shape will remain.

If desired, repeat several times, overlapping the pattern and changing the color of the chalk.

Cut a leaf from **tagboard**.

Roll **fall-colored tissue paper** into balls and **glue** them on the leaf.

Use different colors to create designs and contrast.

Cover the leaf completely.

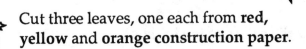

Cut three leaves, one each from **red, yellow** and **orange construction paper**.

Use **yarn** to hang the leaves from a **small branch** to create a fall mobile.

Trace the pattern on **white construction paper**.

Cut squares of **red, orange, yellow tissue paper**.

Apply the squares, overlapping, with **starch** and a **paintbrush**.

After the starch dries, use **scissors** to cut out around the outline.

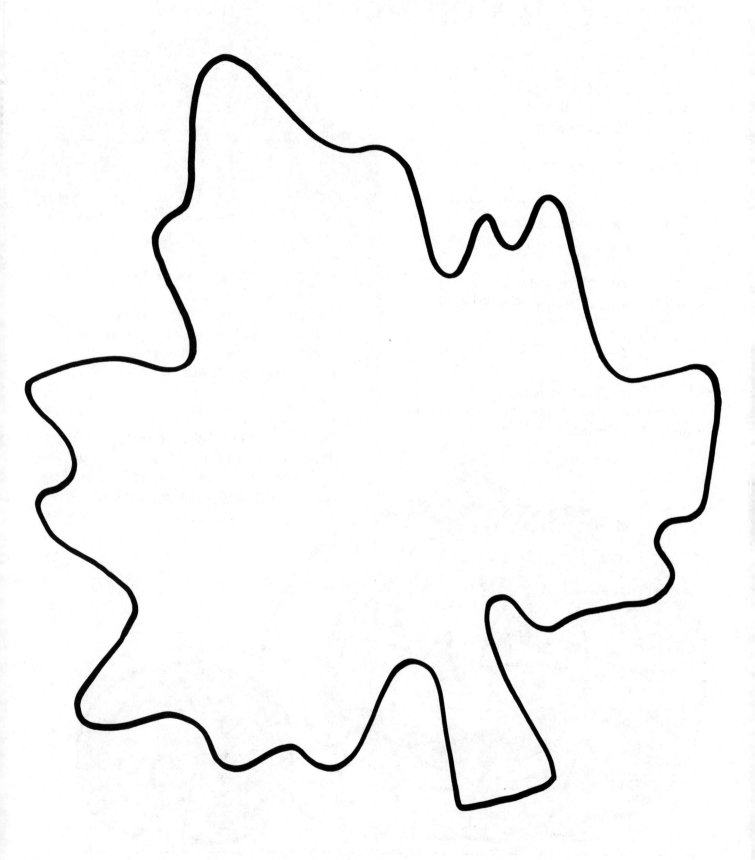

A Pile of Pumpkins

Look Inside!
Pretend you have cut a pumpkin in half.
What would you see?

Recreate that on the pattern.

If you want to make it more elaborate, use
thread and actual pumpkin seeds.

Pumpkins in Disguise
Provide paper, trim, sequins, and glue.
Create a costume for a pumpkin.

Geometric Jack
Only geometric shapes can be used to create
a jack 'o lantern face.

Vocabulary Jacks

Brainstorm a list of words — happy, creepy,
surprised, etc. Choose a word and color a
jack 'o lantern face that fits the descrip-
tion. Classmates try to match the "jack" to
a word.

Personal Pumpkin
Decorate a pumpkin with your own physical features—eye color, hair color, freckles,
glasses, braces, missing teeth, etc.

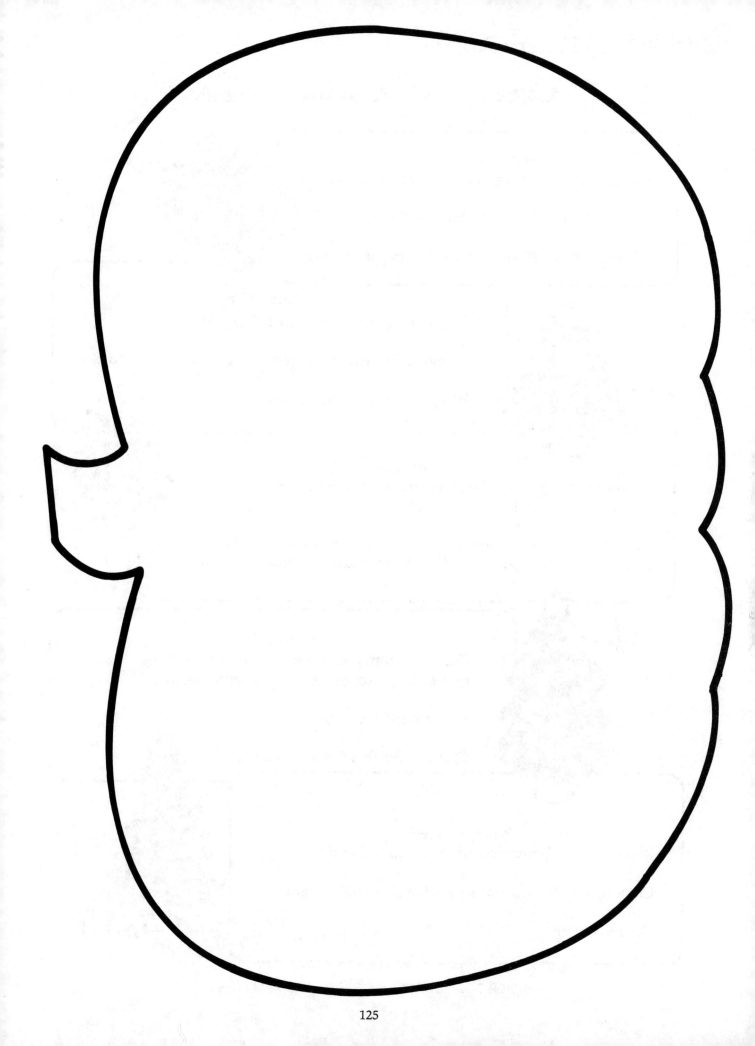

125

A Chorus of Christmas Trees

Ornamental Tree

Cut the **pattern** from **green construction paper**.

Use a **hole punch** to make holes in the tree.

Glue to **red or yellow construction** paper backing.

Flocked Tree

Cut a tree from **green construction paper**.

Sponge paint with **white tempera** to create a flocked effect.

Add **paper** cut out ornaments.

Gift Ideas

Reproduce the **pattern. Color,** cut out with **scissors** and **glue** to a colorful **paper** backing.

Cut out pictures from **magazines** that show what you would like to find under your holiday tree. Glue them under and around the tree.

Fringed Tree

Cut a tree from **green construction paper**. Fringe **tissue paper** strips and **glue** them in rows to the tree.

Trim around the edges.

Glue real **cranberries** for ornaments.

Wrapped Tree

Reproduce the **pattern** on **white construction paper**.

Cut a variety of **Christmas giftwrap** into small sections.

Glue to the tree.

127

Quick and Easy Pattern Projects

So Many Santas

Bearded One

Reproduce pattern. Add a paper hat.

Select from the list of suggestions below to complete Santa's beard:

fringed tissue paper
rolled tissue paper
styrofoam pieces
cotton
torn white material strips

curled construction paper
string dipped in white paint/glue mixture
flour sprinkled on thin glue
sponge paint
soap flake mixture

Santa's New Hat

Reproduce and cut out pattern. Design a new hat for Santa. Color, cut or paint and glue to his head. Here are suggestions:

cowboy
tam-o'shanter
beret
straw
sailor
and so on...

Santa Standup

Fold a round paper plate in half.

Cut out the Santa pattern, color, add a hat and glue to one half of the paper plate. (The beard should not extend below the plate.)

Santa will stand up as a center piece.

Quick & Easy Pattern Projects

A Handful of Hearts

Patchwork Heart Throbs

Cut the large heart from **white or pastel construction paper.**

Use a **ruler** and **black crayon** or **marker** to divide the heart into sections. Make short crayon marks across the lines to resemble stitching.

Fill in each section. Here are suggestions:
  classmates' autographs
  pictures of friends and family
  pictures or descriptions of things that
  make your heart "throb"

Heart Wreath

Cut six large and six small hearts from **contrasting paper, giftwrap** or **doilies.**

Assemble them as shown, on a **construction paper** backing. **Glue** to hold. Add **ribbon** bows.

Heart Pins

Make this pin to give to a special someone.

Cut two small hearts from **felt** or **construction paper.** Decorate with **trims**—lace, sequins, buttons.

Connect the hearts with one length of **ribbon.** Tie the ribbon in a bow in the center.

Attach a **safety pin** to the bow.

Message from the Heart

Cut one large and one small heart from both **construction paper** and **tagboard.**

Glue the paper to the tagboard to cover. Glue a **clothespin** to the large heart and the small heart to the clothespin.

Send a "heartfelt" message to a friend.

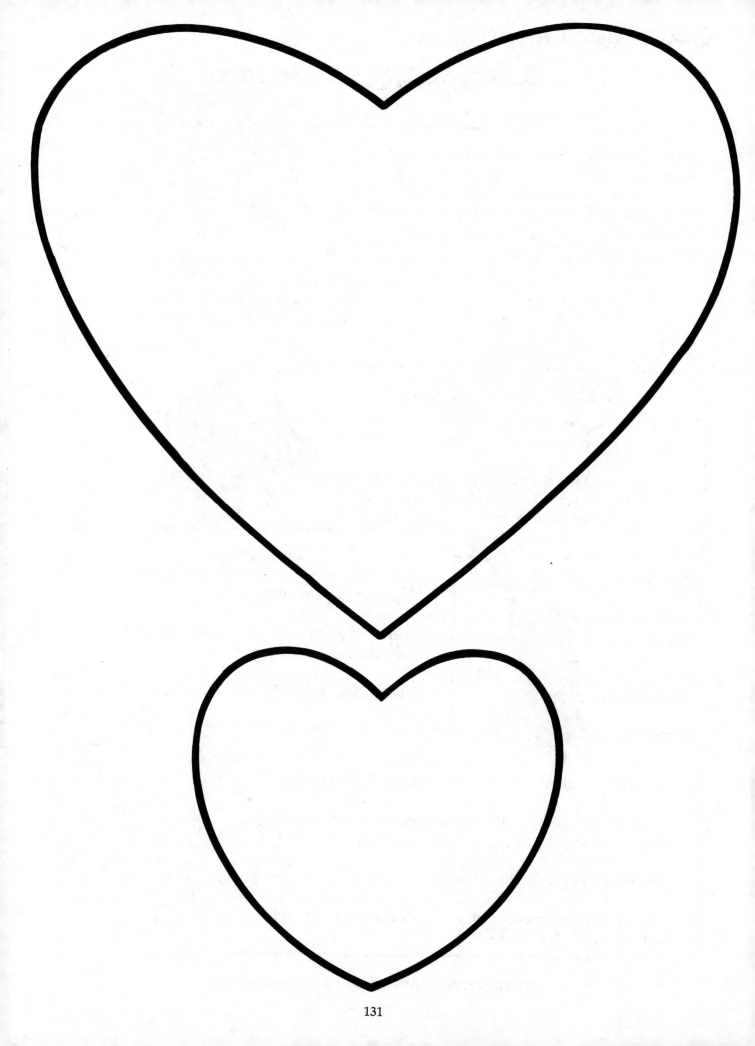

Quick & Easy Pattern Projects

Shamrock Showcase

Outlines
Reproduce the shamrock on **white paper**. Use **crayons** or **markers** to repeat the shamrock's outline at intervals until the center is reached.

Green Things
Make a collage of green things cut from **magazine pictures**. **Glue** them to a cut-out shamrock shape.

St. Patrick's Day Symbols
Start with a green shamrock **glued** to the center of a larger sheet of **construction paper**.

Color around the shamrocks with things that remind you of St. Patrick's Day—rainbow, pot of gold, potatoes from Ireland, leprechauns, mushrooms.

Layered Look
Cut two shamrocks from different shades of green **construction paper**.

Overlap and **glue** the shamrocks to a larger sheet of construction paper.

Glue **yarn** in an outline around each shamrock.

Shamrock Cut Outs
Cut a shamrock from **construction paper**. Fold in half.

Beginning at the fold follow the shape and cut out a smaller shamrock.

Repeat with the new shamrock.

Arrange on construction paper and **glue** in place. Sprinkle with **green glitter**.

Easter Egg Extravaganza

Egg Outlines
Cut eggs from fabric or patterned giftwrap. Glue to construction paper. Glue yarn around each egg to outline.

Egg Hatch
Cut out the large egg from construction paper. Cut it in half with a zig-zag cut. Glue the halves to construction paper. Color a picture of a newly hatched chick. Glue small scraps of white paper around the chick to look like eggshell pieces.

Easter Wreath
Cut out 14 small eggs from assorted colors of construction paper.

Overlap and glue togethr to form a wreath. Glue a pretty spring bow to the top.

Egg-centric People
Cut out an assortment of large and small eggs. Glue them together on paper backing to form people.

Add yarn hair, facial features, etc.

Seasonal Celebrations

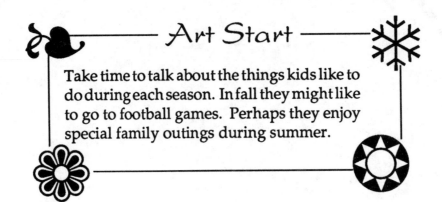

Art Start

Take time to talk about the things kids like to do during each season. In fall they might like to go to football games. Perhaps they enjoy special family outings during summer.

Seasonal Circles

Things you'll need:

- white construction paper circle, 7" in diameter
- 8" square construction paper, any color
- crayons • brad

Directions:

1. Divide the circle into four equal sections.
2. Label each corner of the square with the name of a season.
3. Students draw a picture of something they like to do during the season in the four circle sections.
4. Attach the circle to the square with a brad through the center.
5. Exchange the seasonal circles with classmates to see if they can turn the circle and match the picture to the season.

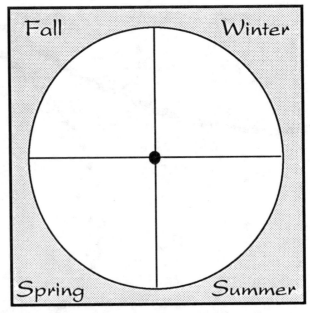

Tree Transformations

Things you'll need:
- white construction paper
- watercolors • brush

Art Start

Talk about the changes in nature that can be seen from one season to the next.

Directions:

1. Fold the paper into four sections.
2. Paint a tree trunk in each section.
3. Add details to show how the same tree might look throughout the year—red and orange leaves during fall, bare branches during winter, blossoms in spring and full summer bloom.

Door Ornaments

Pick a season and make a door ornament
to welcome guests to your home.

Fall
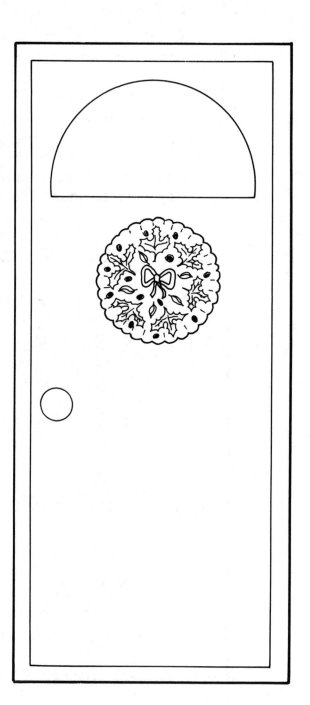

Glue together several corn husks in a
fan shape. Glue pods or fall foliage to
the husks. Tie with a ribbon.

Winter

Tie together pine needles with a red
bow. Sponge paint with white paint
for a snowy effect.

Spring

Glue bright green leaves to a paper
plate. use fingertips to add pretty
flower buds.

Summer

Tie together branches of dried wild
flowers. Tie with a pastel bow.

SEASONAL WINDOWS

Create a mural that depicts a seasonal scene.

Follow the display suggestion then sit back and pretend you're inside, looking out at the world!

— Art Start —

Make this a cooperative learning experience.

Divide into groups. Discuss what they want to appear in their mural, what medium—crayon, paint, construction paper—they will use.

Make decisions regarding preparation and cleanup.

Directions:

Teacher Preparation

Provide each group with a large sheet of butcher paper. Once they have determined the medium they want to use (see Art Start above) help them assemble the necessary materials.

Display

When the murals are finished, tack them to the wall. Cut long black strips of butcher paper and tack over the murals to simulate a window.

— Variation —

This can be an individual project if done on a large sheet of construction paper. Cut window frames from black paper and glue in place over finished scene.

"FALL" ING LEAVES

Here are four projects sure to bring the crisp feel of fall into your classroom.

SPATTER PAINTING

THINGS YOU'LL NEED:

- powdered tempera paint
- cheesecloth or gauze
- construction paper
- rubberband
- flat leaves (or leaf pattern)
- spray bottle filled with water

DIRECTIONS:

1. Wet the construction paper with the spray bottle.

2. Lay the two to three leaves on the construction paper in an overlapping pattern.

3. Put powdered tempera in a folded piece of cheesecloth and close the top with a rubberband.

4. Shake the dry paint gently over the paper.

5. Allow to dry then remove the leaves.

TORN LEAVES

Torn paper shapes easily resemble leaves when glued to paper either on a painted branch, falling from a branch or stacked in a pile ready to be raked. Plus the tearing action provides good small motor skill practice.

Be sure to use fall colors!

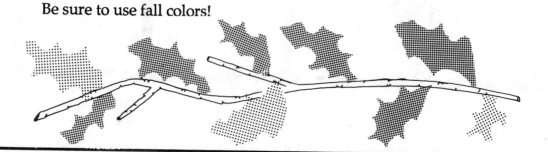

EASY TISSUE PRINTS

Tear **tissue paper** into leaf shapes. Dampen the tissue with a **sponge** dipped in **water**. Allow to dry. Peel the tissue off—the color will remain.

Paint the back of some real leaves with **brown tempera**. Press them over the tissue designs.

Or as a variation, make a leaf print on tissue paper. When the print has dried tear the tissue paper around the leaf shape. Apply with brushed-on starch to a construction paper backing.

BEGINNER'S LEAF PRINTS

THINGS YOU'LL NEED:

- fresh leaves
- white construction paper
- tempera paint mixed with starch (3-5 colors)
- paintbrush

DIRECTIONS:

1. Use a brush to spread a small amount of paint over the back of a leaf.

2. Press the painted side of the leaf on the construction paper. Carefully rub it with your fingers.

3. Repeat the procedure, varying the colors and shapes of leaves.

Skate

Into Winter

┌───────────────── *Things You'll Need:* ─────────────────┐

- four 9"x12" white construction paper
- newspaper • yarn
- hole punch • stapler
- skate pattern (following) • crayons

└──┘

Directions:

1. Reproduce four skates on the white paper for each student.

2. Color and cut out the skates. Be sure that opposite sides are colored when skates are paired.

3. Cut out area between blade and shoe.

4. Match two skates. Glue the blades together.

5. Punch holes on the black circles. Staple the shoe on all sides except for the punched area.

6. Lightly stuff the skate with newspaper or tissue.

7. Lace the holes with yarn and tie in a bow on top.

8, Connect the skates with another length of yarn.

┌───────────────── *Followup Fun* ─────────────────┐

Make a list of winter sports. Find out about the equipment needed for each. Plan a "Winter Sport" day. Bring in pictures to share of winter sport activities, view a movie about skiing, write about a favorite sport, and enjoy some snow cones!

└──┘

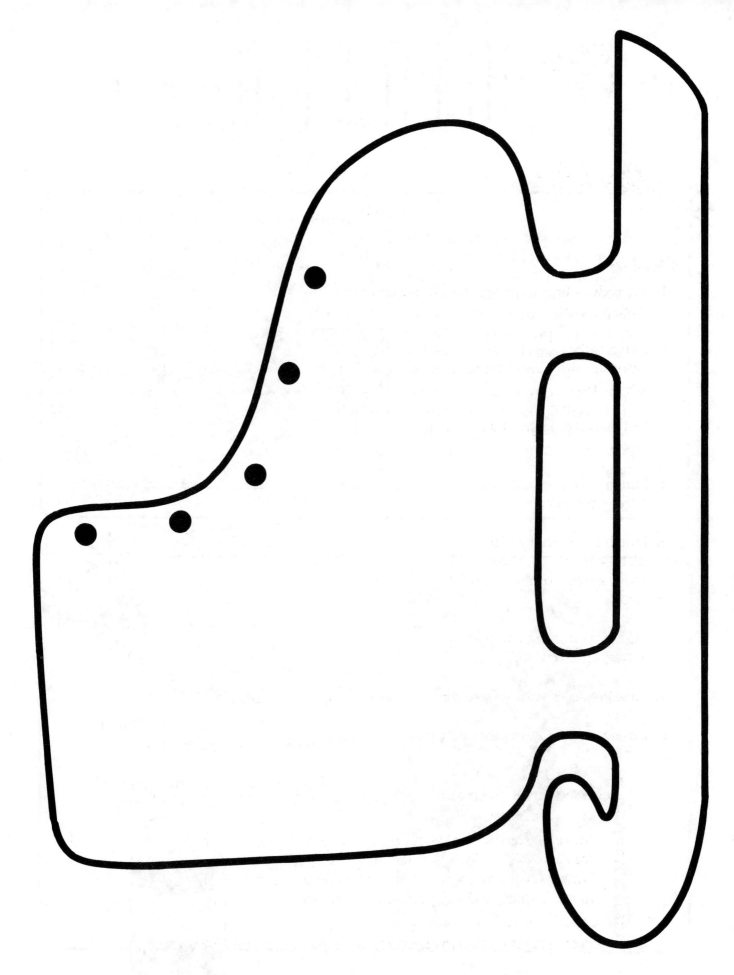

Easy W I N T E R Scenes

Place a **dark sheet of construction paper** on top of a large piece of **newspaper.** Use a bottle of **glue** as paint to make a simple picture on the dark sheet of paper. For solid areas of the picture, spread the glue with your finger.

Sprinkle **salt** over the glue, covering it well. Shake off the excess salt over the newspaper. Let the picture dry completely before hanging it up.

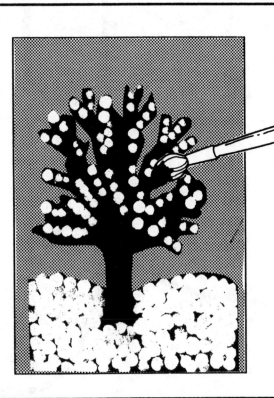

Paint a bare winter tree with **black paint** on **blue paper.**

Use **cotton swabs** dipped in **white paint** to create a snowscene.

TEMPERA PAINT

Berry Basket Snowflakes

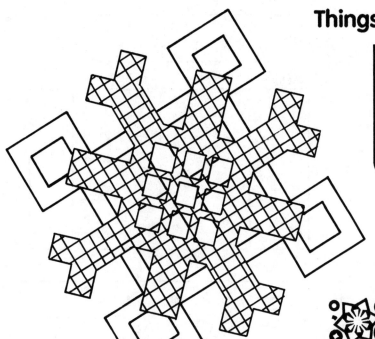

Things You'll Need:

- plastic berry baskets
- scissors
- silver spray paint
- glue
- ribbon or yarn

Directions:

1. Cut the bottoms from the berry baskets. (You can cut out parts of the grillwork to make pretty patterns).

2. Use each bottom alone or glue two together at an angle.

3. Spray with silver paint.

4. When dry, hang each snowflake with a piece of ribbon or pretty yarn.

Frosty the Snowman

Things You'll Need:

- large sheet blue construction paper
- half sheet (lengthwise cut, 6"x18") white construction paper
- various colors construction paper scraps
- glue • scissors

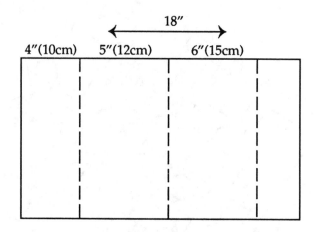

Directions:

1. Cut white paper as shown.

2. Roll white construction paper into tubes. Glue to hold.

3. Glue tubes, smallest width at the top, to build a snowman on the blue paper. Glue the tubes to each other, too.

4. Use construction paper to add detail to background and snowman—facial features (corncob pipe, button nose), scarf, broom, hat, sun, snowbank, sled, etc.

SNOWFLAKE SNOWMEN

THINGS YOU'LL NEED:

- large sheet of white tissue paper
- dark colored construction paper (for background)
- scissors • glue (diluted)
- paintbrush • watercolors

DIRECTIONS:

1. Cut three tissue circles, in graduated sizes.

2. Fold the circles in half several times and make cut out shapes along the folds, as if making snowflakes.

3. Glue the snowflake circles to the background paper, the smallest at the top. (Paint the glue on the tissue.)

4. Cut tissue paper scraps for an easy collage background. Select winter colors—shades of blue, gray, black and white.

VARIATION

Younger students may use several doilies instead of cutting tissue snowflakes.

APRIL SHOWERS

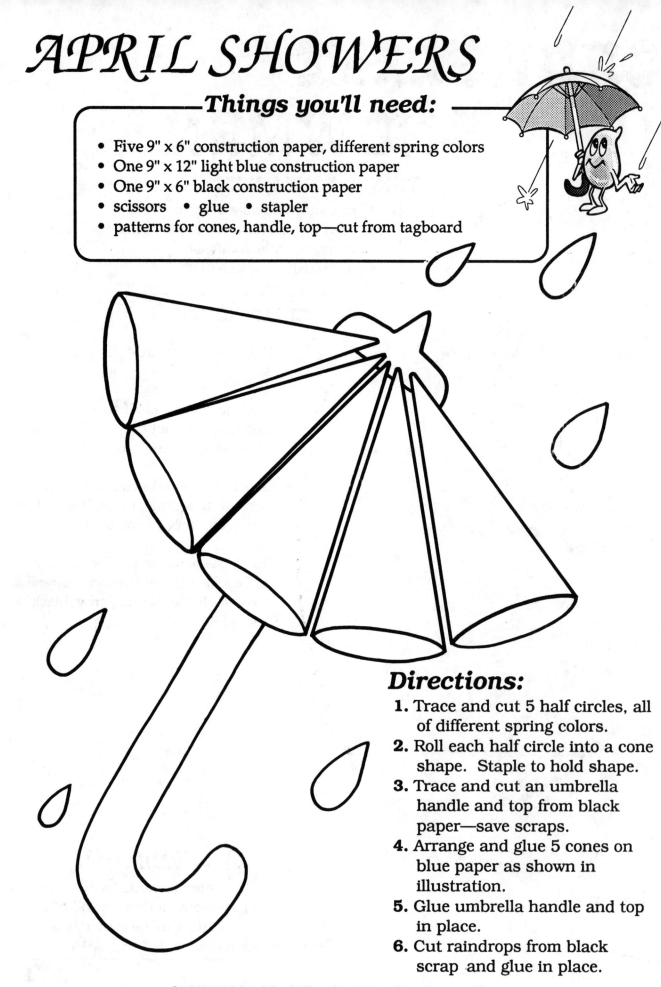

Things you'll need:

- Five 9" x 6" construction paper, different spring colors
- One 9" x 12" light blue construction paper
- One 9" x 6" black construction paper
- scissors • glue • stapler
- patterns for cones, handle, top—cut from tagboard

Directions:

1. Trace and cut 5 half circles, all of different spring colors.
2. Roll each half circle into a cone shape. Staple to hold shape.
3. Trace and cut an umbrella handle and top from black paper—save scraps.
4. Arrange and glue 5 cones on blue paper as shown in illustration.
5. Glue umbrella handle and top in place.
6. Cut raindrops from black scrap and glue in place.

Spring Flowers

Here's a "bouquet" of flower patterns for creating lifelike displays in your classroom.

Art Start

Look through flower catalogs and books. Research accurate color and detail

Display

Tack yarn in a wavy ground line along the wall.

"Plant" flowers along the ground line.

Create stems from rolled paper or paper strips.

Technique Tip

Make samples so that children have a visual guide. Most of the flowers are most effective if made from construction paper. Exceptions are noted and color suggestions are given.

Sweet Peas

Colors: pink, white, purple

Cut from crepe paper.

1. Cut two petals for each flower. The grain of the crepe paper should run up and down (wide to narrow part of the petal).

2. Lay the two petals on top of each other. Lay a length of green wire across the petals and fold the pointed end up and over the wire. Pull the wire together and twist to form a stem.

3. Fluff the petals.

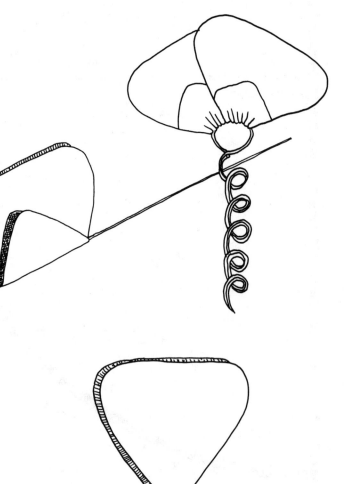

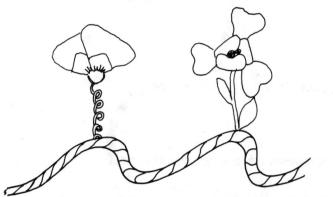

These two flowers begin with the same pattern.

Tulip

Colors: all

1. Cut out the pattern.

2. Overlap the petals slightly and glue to hold, forming a cup.

Iris

Colors: all
(Iris means "rainbow" in Greek.)

1. Cut out the pattern.

2. Pull every other petal toward the center and glue to hold.

3. Curl down the remaining three petals.

Lily

Colors: reddish-orange or white

1. Cut out pattern.

2. Curl petals over a pencil.

3. Roll into a cone, curled petals out, and glue closed with the tab on the outside.

Daffodil

Colors: yellow

1. Cut out the patterns. Curl the center petals around a pencil.

2. Roll the center into a cone, tab on the inside, smaller tabs folded out. Glue to hold shape.

3. Glue the center tabs to the larger petal shape.

Cherry Blossom Time

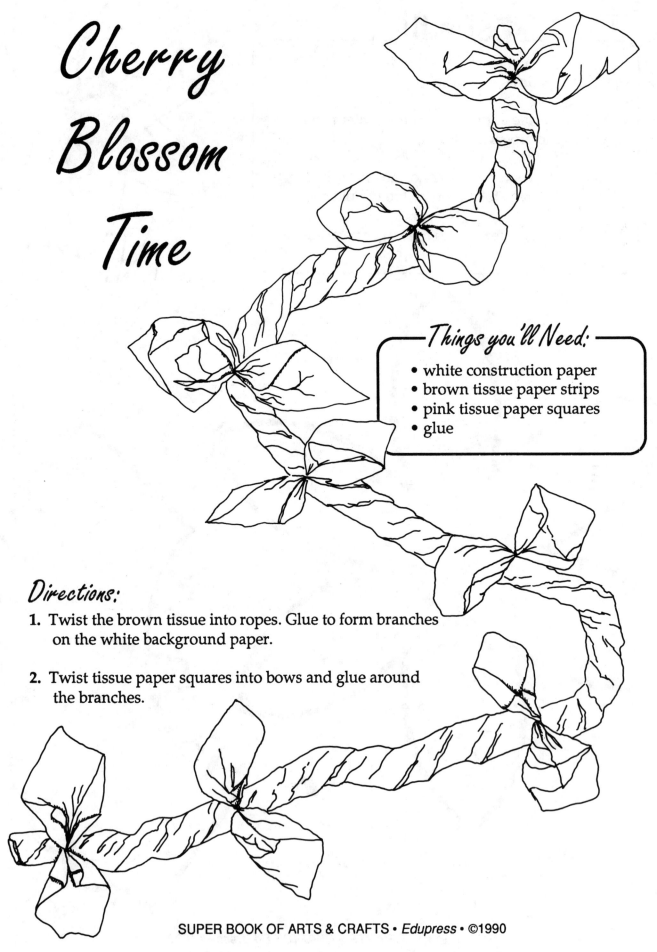

Directions:

1. Twist the brown tissue into ropes. Glue to form branches on the white background paper.

2. Twist tissue paper squares into bows and glue around the branches.

Blooming Garden

Things You'll Need:

- one 12"x18" light blue construction paper
- cotton balls
- four to six paper baking cups
- crayons • glue
- pebbles

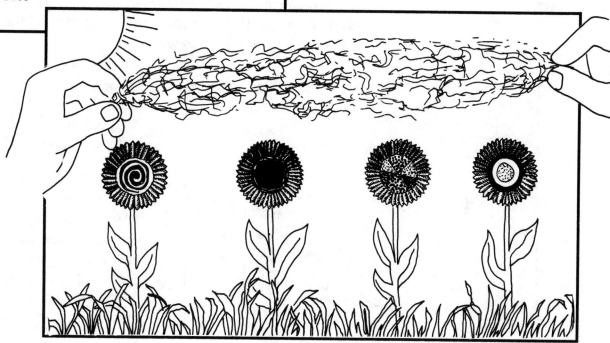

Directions:

1. Color a garden scene. Include green grass and a sun. Color just the stems and leaves of four to six flowers. Space them across the page.

2. Glue a baking cup "flower" to the top of each stem. Color the center of each flower.

3. Glue cotton ball clouds. Stretch them out to make them wispy.

4. Glue a few pebbles among the blades of grass.

Colorful Flowerpot

Things you'll Need:
- 12"x18" white construction paper
- newspaper
- crayons
- watercolors

Directions:

1. Tear five freeform shapes from newspaper. Each will be different. Place them on the construction paper and trace around each lightly with crayon.

2. Color a stamen in the center of each flower shape. Use several colors in an expanding circle.

3. Create petals by using black crayon to draw lines from the stamen to the outer edge of the flower. The lines should be curvy and the petals uneven in size.

4. Color the remainder of the flower heavily with bright colors.

5. Create a vase or bowl below the flowers. Draw stems from the vase to each flower. Add leaves.

6. Paint over the entire picture with a water-color wash.

Geometric Flowers

The center of each flower is a geometric shape!

Things You'll Need:

- one 12"x18" white construction paper
- crayons
- black marker or crayon
- geometric patterns (teacher-made, cut from cardboard)—square, oval, diamond, circle, rectangle

Directions:

1. Choose three geometric patterns—all the same or different—to trace on the white construction paper.

2. Color the traced shape with a design or pattern.

3. Surround the shape with various-shaped petals. Color heavily to achieve bright tones.

4. Draw leaves and stems. Color the background solid.

5. Outline with a black marking pen.

BIG, BIG Blossoms

Things You'll Need:
- paper plate
- construction paper
- scissors • pencil
- brad • glue
- green tempera paint • paint brush

Directions:

1. Paint the paper plate green.

2. Cut three to five graduated-sized construction paper circles. (Older students can use a compass.) The largest circle should be the same size as the paper plate.

3. Cut petal shapes around the edge of each circle. They can be the same or different. Here are some suggested shapes.

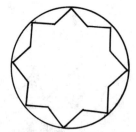  

4. Curl the petals around a pencil toward the center.

5. Attach the flowers to the paper plate with a brad through the center. Begin with the largest and end with the smallest. You may want to glue them in place.

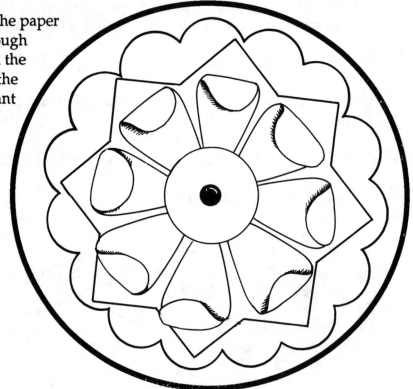

Flower Explosions

Things You'll Need:

- white, black and bright construction paper
- marking pens • glue • scissors
- sponge squares

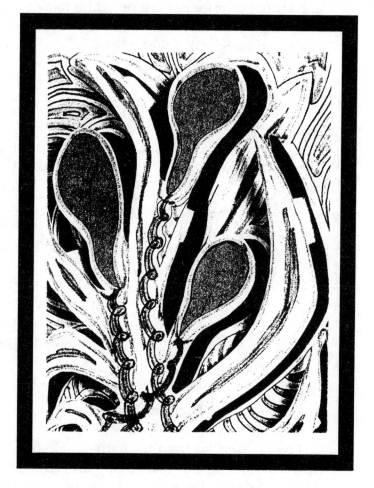

Directions:

1. Cut one to three bold blossoms from bright construction paper.

2. Glue the blossoms to white construction paper.

3. Use marking pens to draw stems and leaves for each blossom.

4. Outline the entire flower—stem, leaves and blossom, with marking pens in contrasting colors, beginning at the flower and finishing near the edge of the paper.

5. Cut out the original flower (stem and leaves, too). Glue the remaining background to a larger piece of contrasting paper.

6. Glue small sponge squares to the back of each flower. Glue the flowers in their original position. The flowers should "pop out" at you.

Butterflies Are Everywhere

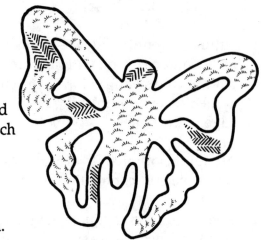

Here are some butterfly projects using the pattern at right for the young and old alike!

Glittering Wings

Reproduce butterfly **pattern** on **white paper.** color each section with **crayons.** Paint **diluted glue** over isolated areas. Sprinkle with **glitter.**

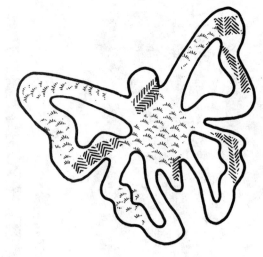

Marbled Butterflies

Reproduce the **pattern** on **white paper.** Place the entire page in a **shallow box.** Scatter several dabs of various colored **tempera** around the butterfly pattern.

Place **two marbles** in the box and roll them back and forth. The paint will be tracked over the butterfly.

Allow the paint to dry. Younger students can outline the butterfly with a bright marker. Older students can cut them out and remount them to contrasting construction paper.

Hanging Butterfly

Cut two butterflies from the **pattern.** On one, bend **thin wire** and **tape** in place along the outline of each wing and down the center of the butterfly.

Glue the second pattern over the first.

Bend wings into desired position. Hang with **yarn.**

LACY BUTTERFLIES

DIRECTIONS:

1. Cut a doily in half.

2. Glue the halves to brightly colored construction paper, separating them slightly.

3. Paint a body between the doily halves.

4. Dab various colors of paint on the doily "wings".

5. Cut the paper around the doily, leaving a border

Summer
Sand 'n Sails

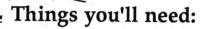

Things you'll need:

- One 4 1/2" x 5 1/2" piece fine sandpaper
- One 4 1/2" x 5 1/2" piece white construction paper
- One 5" x 12" piece colored construction paper
- crayons • glue • iron

Directions:

1. Draw a simple boat onto the sandpaper with crayon. Heavily color all parts of the sketch, including the background.

2. Put white construction paper directly over the sandpaper.

3. Press a medium-heated iron over white paper. (Do not move the iron back and forth.)

4. Carefully lift off the white paper. A crayon imprint will transfer from the sandpaper.

5. Glue the two pictures side by side on the larger piece of construction paper. There should be a border on all sides.

SUNS IN A SNAP

Heat up your classroom with these easy, "sunny" projects.

Looped Sun

Paste a large yellow or orange circle on contrasting paper.

Make loops from strips of sun-colored construction paper.

Paste the ends closed. Paste the loops around the circle.

Torn Rays

Start with an orange circle glued to white construction paper.

Tear orange, red and yellow rays from construction paper. Glue around the circle.

Red-Hot Sun

Sponge paint an orange background on white construction paper.

Mix red tempera paint and glue.

Squeeze a sun onto the background. Allow glue mixture to dry thoroughly.

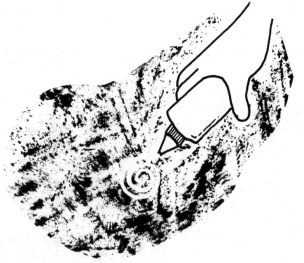

Bears on the Beach

Things You'll Need:

- white and brown construction paper
- fabric
- paint
- glue
- scissors
- sponge or paint brush
- construction paper scraps

Directions:

1. Sponge paint or brush the background—water, sand, sky, sun.

2. Use the pattern below to trace and cut one to three bears from brown construction paper.

3. Cut fabric swimming trunks or bathing suits to fit the bears. (If fabric is not available, cut from white paper and decorate.)

4. Assemble bears and clothing and glue to the dry background.

5. Add construction paper detail—umbrella, beach ball, sand bucket, beach chair, whale.

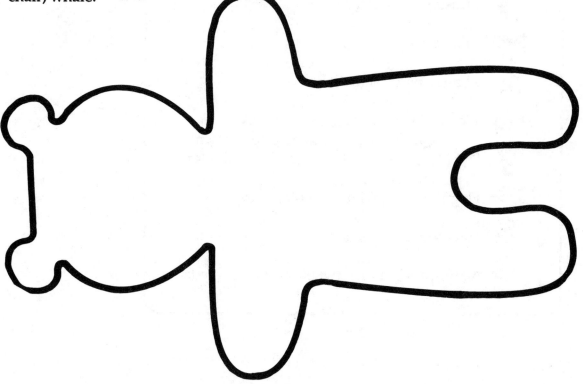

Spiral Mobile

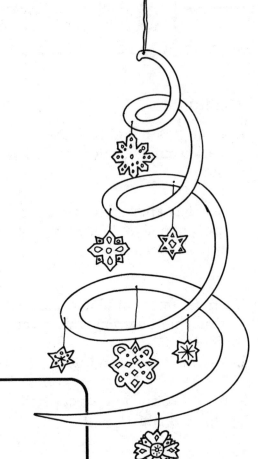

Reproduce the pattern on the following page on any color construction paper.

Cut on the dotted lines.

Punch holes at random intervals and use thread or thin yarn to suspend the objects you have chosen. (They must be light-weight.)

Reinforce the top section with an extra piece of cardboard. Punch a hole through the cardboard and hang the entire mobile with yarn.

Idea Menu

 Christmas: assorted bows

 Fall: leaves

 Winter: tissue snowflakes

 Victoria Day (Canada): silhouettes of Queen Victoria and gold foil crowns.

 President's Day: silhouettes of Washington and Lincoln

 Flag Day: red, white and blue stars

 Halloween: black bats or cats

 Nature celebration: twigs and dried weeds

Spiral Mobile Pattern

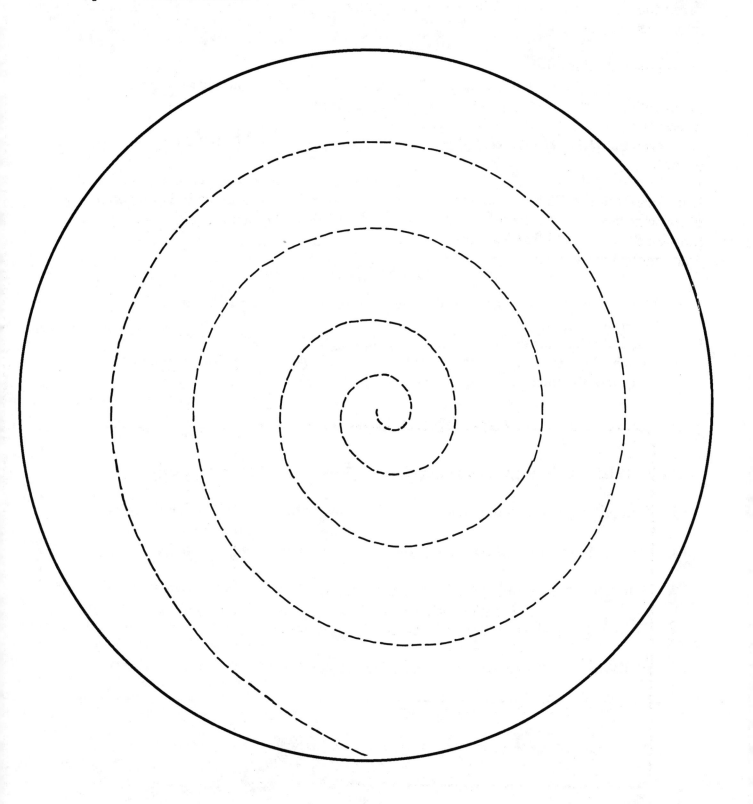

Garland Greetings

Adapt these garlands to any holiday or season and turn your classroom into an instant celebration!

Things you'll need:

- 1 yard (*1 meter*) thick yarn
- construction paper
- scissors   • hole punch
- glue   • thin yarn

Display

Connect individual garlands end to end and drape around classroom walls and bulletin boards.

Directions:

1. Cut (freehand or from a pattern) 5-7 holiday or seasonal shapes—choose from following menu.
2. Decorate shapes, add detail with paint, paper, glitter etc.
3. Punch a hole in the top of each shape and tie with yarn at even intervals along the length of the thick yarn. (Shapes can also be stapled.)

Menu

 Fall Harvest: leaves, fruits, vegetables

 Winter: snowmen, snowflakes

 Spring: flowers

 Summer: sun and sailboats

 Thanksgiving: Pilgrim hats, turkeys

 Halloween: pumpkins, masks

 Valentines Day: hearts

 St. Patricks Day: shamrocks, mushrooms

 Easter: eggs, bunnies

 Victoria Day: crowns, silhouettes

 Fourth of July: red, white, blue bursts

 Presidents' Day: silhouettes

HOLIDAY HANG UPS

Adapt these easy-to-make hangings to any holiday or season. Just choose from the "Material Menu" that follows.

As a special gift for a special someone or for hanging in the classroom, this project is sure to please the eye.

THINGS YOU'LL NEED:

- waxed paper
- construction paper
- stapler • yarn
- iron
- scissors
- paper towels
- variety of materials chosen from Material Menu

DIRECTIONS:

1. Tear off two sheets of waxed paper the same length.
2. Place one sheet on the paper towel, waxed side up. Arrange the material in a random, overlapping design, on the waxed paper.
3. Place the second sheet of waxed paper, waxed side down, over the materials, lining up the edges of both sheets.
4. Use a cool iron to melt the papers together. You may want to lay a paper towel or lightweight dishtowel between the iron and the waxed paper.
5. Fold and staple construction paper strips over each end of the panel. Hang with yarn.

MATERIAL MENU

 Christmas: tinsel, red and green glitter, curling ribbon

 Valentine's Day: doilies, lace, pink and red yarn lengths

St. Patrick's Day: green tissue shamrocks, green yarn, green glitter

Spring: flower petals, pastel yarn or thread

 Winter: torn scraps of white tissue, silver glitter, aluminum foil, soap flakes

 Fall: leaves, scraps of orange, brown and red tissue

 Halloween: pumpkin seeds, black tissue bats, orange yarn

BASIC BASKETS

Things you'll need:

- one gallon size plastic milk or juice container
- permanent markers
- scissors   • hole punch
- ribbon or yarn

Directions:

1. Soak a plastic container in warm, soapy water to clean and soften.
2. Draw a holiday outline on the top third of the container. Use the designs below for outline ideas.
3. Use scissors to cut along the outline.
4. Finish the details using permanent markers.
5. For a special border, punch holes about one inch apart along the top edge.
6. Weave a piece of yarn in and out of the holes.

Bunny

Valentine

Pumpkin

Variations:

Easter—fill the bunny with torn tissue or colored grass, add a cotton tail and use in an egg hunt or set out to be filled with treats.

Valentine—Use as a mailbox or fill with a goodie for a special someone.

Pumpkin—Add a rope handle and take door-to-door for tricks or treats.

HOLIDAY MURALS

Here are more ideas for cooperative group murals for the holidays.
Follow the ART START suggestions on the previous page.

 Columbus Day: painted waves, cut out paper ships and sails, painted land on the horizon.

 Halloween: black cats, bats, witches, monsters in a cemetery scene. Make them dimensional by popping out the bat wings, folding down the witch's hat and adding curled paper cat tails.

 Thanksgiving:
Canadian—harvest scene with painted fields, tissue paper fruit.
American—Pilgrims, Indians, feasting at a large table.

 Christmas: paint Santa's workshop with elves, magazine cut-out toys and Santa.

 St. Patrick's Day: large painted rainbow, pot of gold, lots of green, green tissue paper grass.

 Easter: paper rabbits, paint blob butterflies, mosaic eggs, sponge painted grass.

POSITIVE / NEGATIVE
HOLIDAYS

Here's an easy project, adaptable to many holidays, that's also a good lesson in positive/negative. Color section will vary with the holiday.

Things You'll Need:

- half sheet (9"x12") construction paper
- four - 4 1/2"x6" (11.25x15cm) contrasting color construction paper
- scissors • glue

Directions:

1. Fold the small rectangles in half along the longer side. Choose four shapes related to the holiday and sketch half the shape along the fold, as shown. The shapes need to be symmetrical.

2. Carefully cut out each shape. Glue them to the larger piece of construction paper as shown.

Holiday Possibilities:

 Christmas: tree, bell, holly, ornament

 Halloween: pumpkin, ghost, bat, mask

 Easter: bunny, egg, basket, bow

Holiday Picture Frame

— Things You'll Need: —

- half sheet (9x12) white construction paper
- half sheet (9x12) construction paper in holiday color
- tempera paint mixed with starch
- brushes • glue • scissors

Directions:

1. On white paper, paint a design using the holiday colors of your choice. Allow to dry.

2. Using a pattern or cutting freehand, cut a holiday shape from the contrasting color construction paper.

3. Glue the holiday shape to the colorful holiday background.

A Hand-ful of Holiday Art

Just trace your hands on colorful construction paper. Then cut them out and glue them to a background to make these creative seasonal and holiday art projects.

Thanksgiving Turkey

Cut from brown paper. Add colorful feathers

Make a whole "flock" of turkeys in a barnyard!

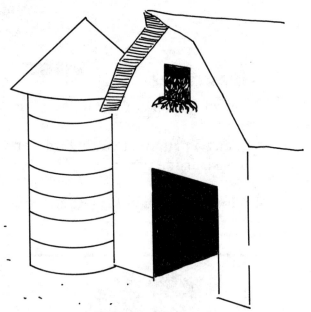

Christmas Tree

Each student cuts a hand from green construction paper.

Curl the fingers around a pencil.

Arrange the hands, fingers pointing down and beginning at the bottom, into a triangular tree shape.

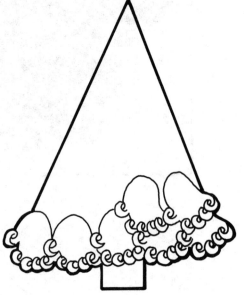

Spring Flowers and Butterflies

Add stems to the flowers and a body to the butterflies!

Spring Tree

Just paint a trunk, add green hands with curled fingers and tissue paper blossoms.

Firework Explosion

Overlap several hands with curled fingers. Sprinkle glitter or spatter paint sparks around the fireworks.

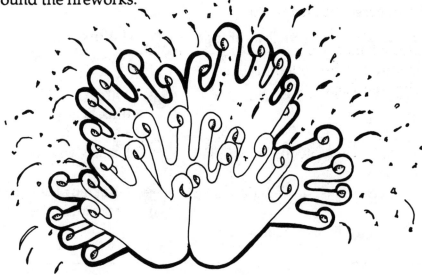

Seasonal Wreath

Things You'll Need:

- 16 ice cream (craft) sticks
- paint (see Material Menu below)
- glue • scissors • ribbon

Directions:

1. Paint the ice cream sticks. Choose a color from the Material Menu below. Paint one side, allow to dry, then paint the other side.

2. Glue two of the sticks together at the center so they form a skinny X. Repeat with all the sticks.

3. Make the wreath by arranging the X's in a circle and gluing them together, end to end.

4. Glue construction paper cutouts (see Material Menu) around the wreath.

5. Tie a piece of ribbon for hanging.

Material Menu

 Fall: brown sticks, red, yellow, orange leaves

 Fall Harvest: brown sticks, fruit and vegetable cutouts

 Winter: white sticks, white snowflakes

 Spring: green sticks, flower cutouts

 Summer: orange sticks, yellow suns

 Halloween: black sticks, white ghosts

 Valentines Day: red sticks, purple, pink hearts

 Easter: yellow sticks, white bunnies

 Fourth of July: red, white, blue sticks and stars

FRACTURED SYMBOLS

Take any holiday symbol pattern or shape
and turn it into a quick and easy art project.

Things You'll Need:

- construction paper (color choice depends on the holiday)
- scissors • glue

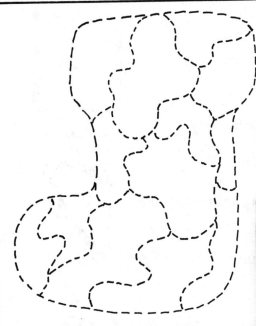

Directions:

1. Use a pattern or freehand cut a large holiday shape from construction paper.

2. Cut the pattern into "puzzle" pieces.

3. Glue the shape back together on a contrasting color construction paper. Leave some space between each piece.

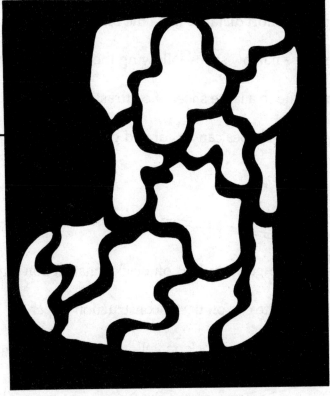

Holiday Cut Outs

Use the Quick and Easy Patterns for these projects or let kids cut their own.

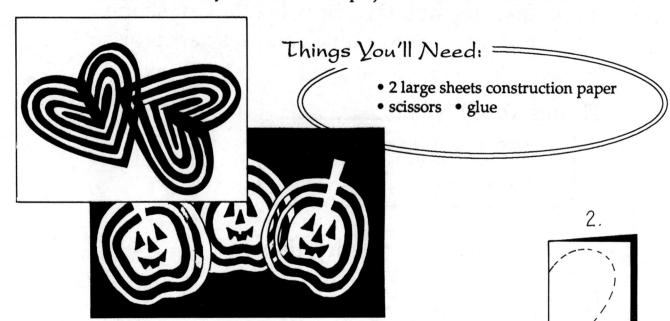

Things You'll Need:

- 2 large sheets construction paper
- scissors • glue

Directions:

1. Select construction paper in contrasting colors to suit the holiday.

2. Cut a large holiday shape from one sheet of folded paper.

3. Keep the paper folded. Cut out a narrow strip, beginning at the bottom and ending a short distance from the fold.

4. Cut two more narrow strips following the same procedure.

5. Open and glue to a large sheet of contrasting paper.

Optional: Several shapes can be cut and glued in an overlapping pattern.

2.

3.

4.

Variations

 orange pumpkins on black construction paper for **Halloween**

white egg on pastel construction paper for **Easter**

green shamrock on yellow construction paper for **St. Patrick's Day**

Things you'll need:

- popsicle sticks
- tempera paint in holiday colors
- fine brushes
- yarn

Directions:

1. Paint popsicle sticks.
2. Glue sticks together in one of the designs illustrated below.
3. Paint sticks on both sides with small dots or designs.
4. Tie yarn around the sticks to hang.

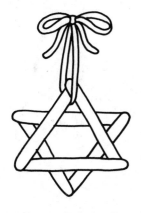

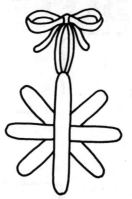

Balanced design

Star of David

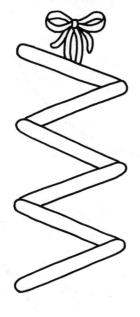

Christmas tree

6 sticks

DIRECTIONS:

1. Reproduce this page on **white construction paper**.
2. Use **crayons** to color the sail emblem red and the ship brown.
3. Use **scissors** to cut out the patterns.
4. **Glue** the ship to a sea of blue waves on a **light blue construction paper** background.

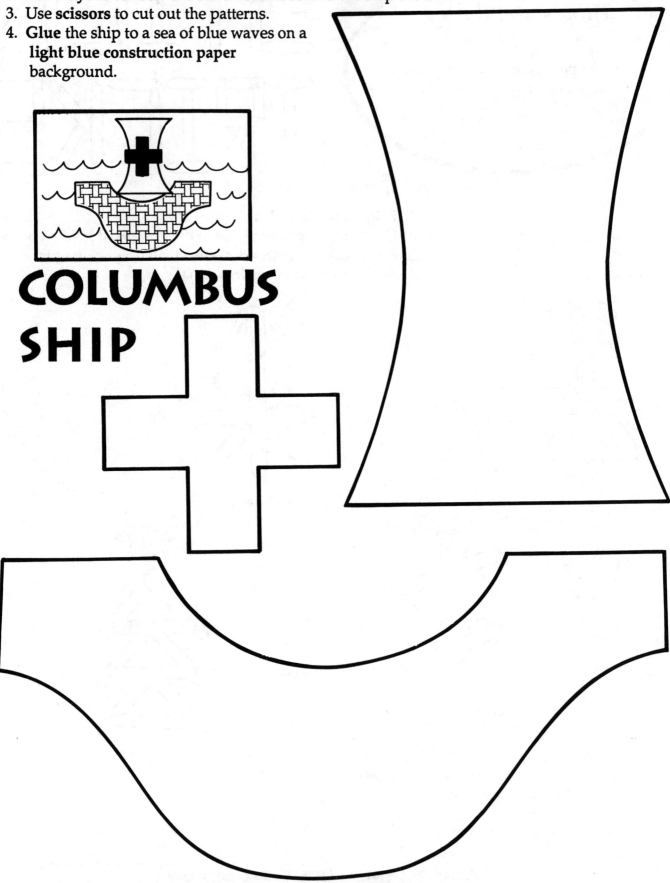

COLUMBUS SHIP

Antiqued Pumpkins

Things You'll Need:

- manila paper
- orange construction paper
- orange and black crayons
- glue • scissors

Directions:

1. Cut a large pumpkin from manila paper.

2. Cut the orange construction paper into very small pieces.

3. Color a heavy black jack-o'-lantern face on the pumpkin. (Or color a yellow face and the pumpkin will appear to be lit.)

4. Glue the orange paper pieces at random intervals on the pumpkin.

5. Color heavily with orange crayon between the glued paper pieces.

6. Brush over the entire pumpkin with a black watercolor wash.

── Variations ──

 pink paper pieces, lime crayon, yellow wash on an Easter egg.

 white paper pieces, green crayon, white wash on a snowy tree.

 lime green paper pieces, yellow crayon, dark green wash on a shamrock

Pumpkin Rollups

Make a large version to use as a table centerpiece. Make smaller versions to use as napkin rings to decorate a holiday table.

Directions:

Cut a large sheet of **orange construction paper** into thirds. The finished size should be 6" (15 cm) x 12" (30 cm).

Decorate one end with a **black crayon** "jack-o-lantern" face.

Roll the length of the orange paper strip until the ends overlap slightly. **Staple or glue** in place. Add a **green paper** stem.

Things you'll Need:

- orange construction paper
- green construction paper
- brown construction paper
- green yarn
- scissors • glue

Directions:

1. Glue a long strand of yarn across a large sheet of brown construction paper.

2. Glue several shorter strands of yarn extending from the first one.

3. Cut pumpkins in various shapes and sizes. Glue them to the yarn vines.

4. Cut green leaves to glue to the vine too.

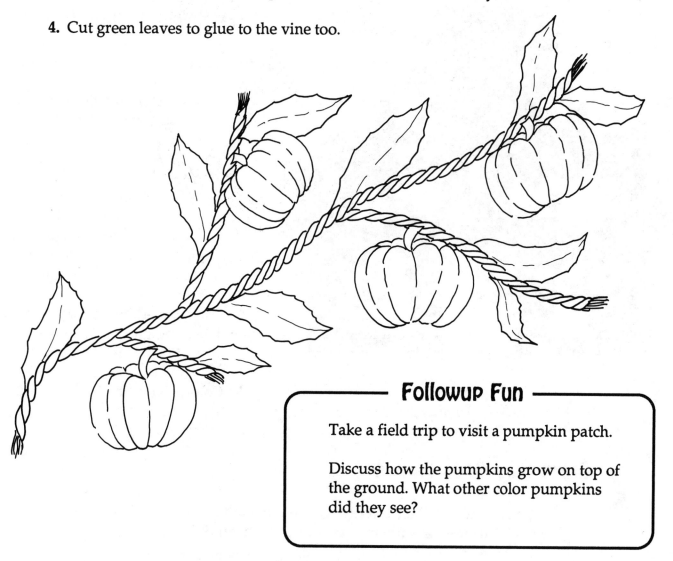

Followup Fun

Take a field trip to visit a pumpkin patch.

Discuss how the pumpkins grow on top of the ground. What other color pumpkins did they see?

Step inside this all-occasion house. The pattern follows.

Things you'll need:

- assorted colors construction paper
- scissors • crayons

Halloween Open House

1. Use the pattern to cut a spooky black house.

2. Cut windows and doors, leaving one side attached so they can open and close.

3. Glue the house to a large piece of white or yellow construction paper. Be sure the openings aren't glued.

4. Draw something spooky—bat, skeleton, black cat, ghost—behind each opening.

5. Color a haunting background.

Christmas Open House

Follow the same instructions but instead cut out a red house and put Christmas scenes—wreath, tree, candle, gift—behind the openings.

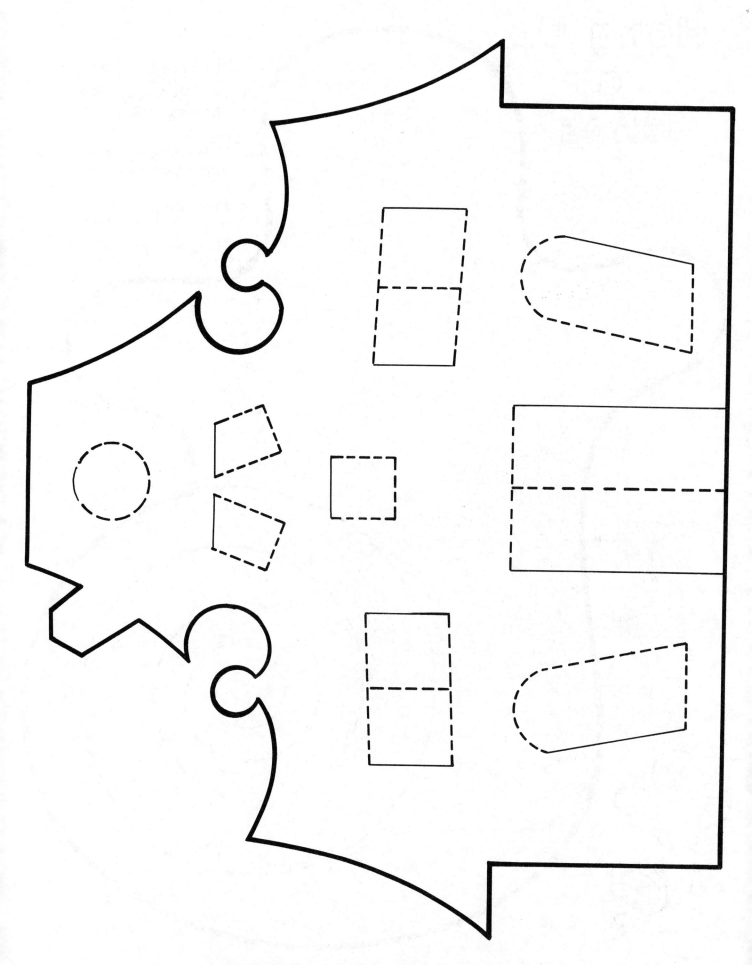

Hang Up a Ghost

What to do:

1. Reproduce ghost on white drawing paper.

2. Cut on outer lines, continuing on dotted lines.

3. Color a face.

4. Hang with yarn.

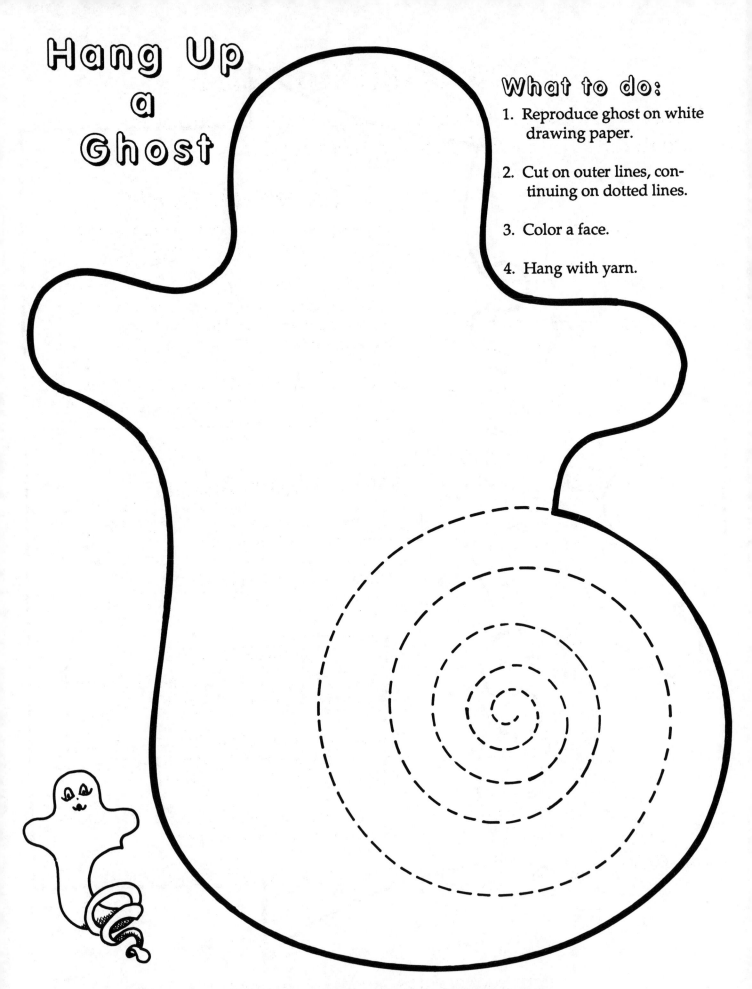

Good Grief! Ghosts!

Here's a bevy of ghosts sure to haunt any classroom. The materials you need for each project appear in **bold** print.

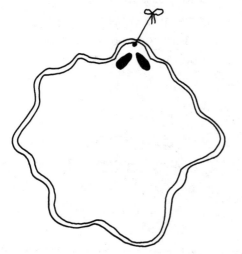

Tissue Paper Ghosts

Run a squiggle line of **glue** on **white tissue paper**. Any shape will do as long as it is a closed shape.

Allow the glue to dry (this may need to set overnight). Use **scissors** to cut out around the glue outline.

Add two black eyes. BOO! A ghost. Hang in the window with **thread**, or glue to a **popsicle stick** for fearless flying!

Ghostly Ghosts

Glue white facial tissue to a large piece of **orange construction paper.**

Add a torn paper head and feet.

Gauzy Ghosts

Dip a 9" x 9" square of **cheesecloth** in a mixture of equal parts **glue** and **water**.

Wring out the excess liquid and drape the cheesecloth over a **small paper cup** or cone shape. Let dry.

Stretch cheesecloth into a ghostly shape. Add **black construction paper** eyes.

Hang with **thread** or glue to a **popsicle stick.**

Things you'll need:

- cornucopia reproduced on white paper
- diluted brown tempera or watercolors
- magazines • scissors • paintbrush

Directions:

1. Paint the cornucopia.
2. Cut out pictures of food from magazines.
3. Glue pictures "spilling" from the cornucopia.

A Couple of Cornucopias

Here are two choices for displaying a Thanksgiving harvest.

Things you'll need:

- 12" x 18" manila construction paper
- various colors tissue paper, including dark brown
- starch • paintbrush • black crayon

Directions:

1. Cut out a brown tissue paper cornucopia.
2. Cut out fruits and vegetables in various colors of tissue paper.
3. Brush starch over the manila paper. While wet, place cornucopia and fruit in position on the starch.
4. Allow to dry. Outline the fruit and cornucopia with black crayon.

Patterns A, B, C (following) reproduced as follows:

Things You'll Need:

- Patterns A, B, C (following) reproduced as follows:
  - 2- A on brown construction paper
  - 1- B on red construction paper
  - 1- C on yellow construction paper
- 7" (18cm) square tagboard
- glue • scissors
- construction paper scraps
- tissue paper (optional)

TURKEY CENTERPIECE

1. Cut out all pattern pieces.

2. Glue turkey body pieces together, in the head area, only!

3. Fold up body base along dotted lines toward the outside.

4. Cut on all other lines. Insert the cuts on the feather sections in the cuts on the body section.

5. Glue the folded tabs at the body base to a piece of tagboard. The turkey sections will need to be spaced about 3" (7.5 cm) apart. Be sure the turkey will stand before gluing in place. (Stuff with a sheet of crumpled tissue, to stabilize.)

6. Add features—wattle, eyes, colorful feathers.

Pattern A

Turkey Centerpiece

(Instructions precede)

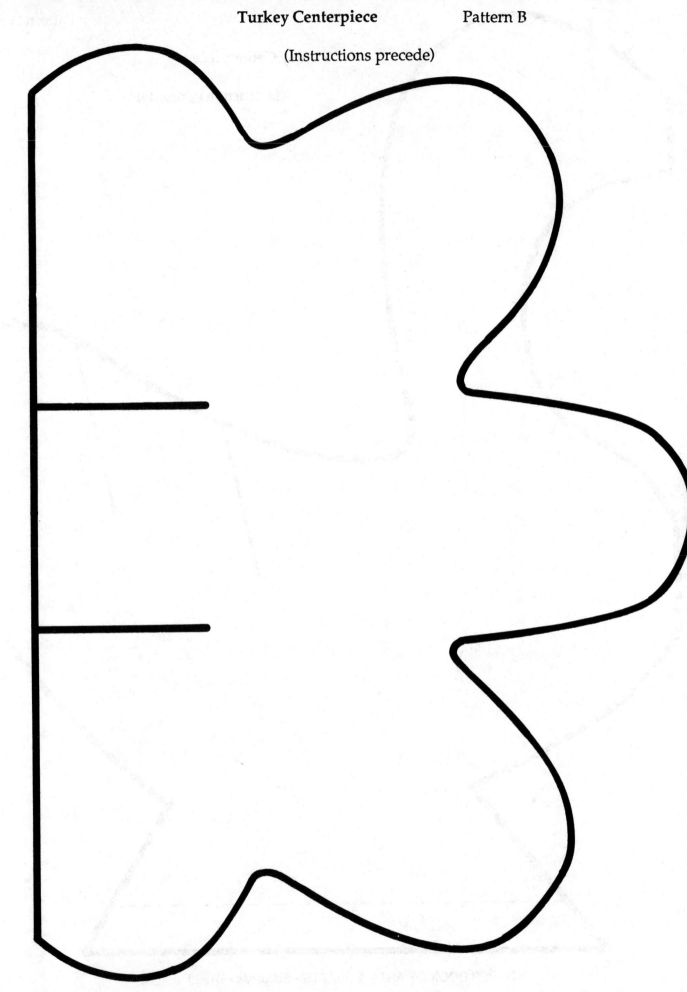

Turkey Centerpiece

(Instructions precede)

Pattern C

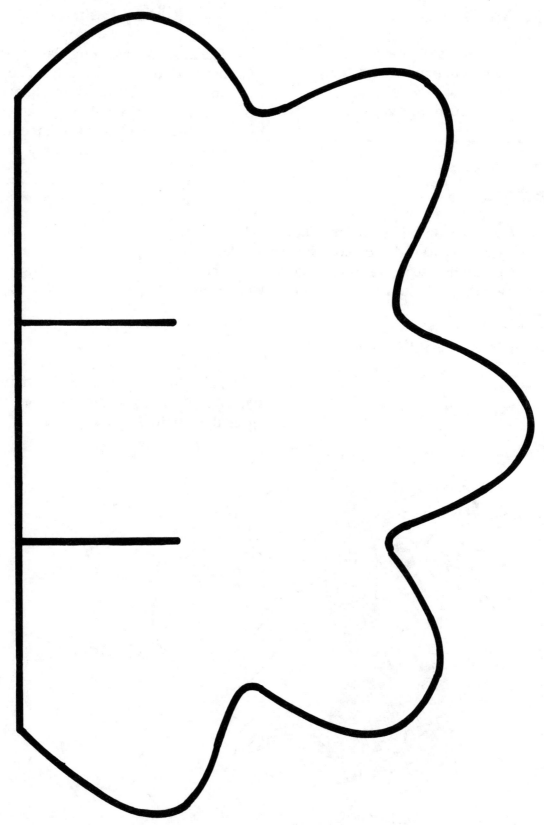

Tube Turkey

Things You'll Need:

- paper towel tube
- tempera paint • brushes
- scissors • glue
- construction paper scraps

Holiday Help

The first Thanksgiving Days were celebrations for plentiful crops. They were, and still are, a time for feasting and sharing. Traditional meals center around a turkey but other main dishes could include venison, duck, goose and fish.

Directions:

1. Cut seven sections of cardboard tubing, each about a half inch (1.5 cm) wide, to make the feet and tail feathers. Cut another section approximately 2 1/2 inches wide for the body, and one about 1 inch wide for the head.

2. Paint the cardboard sections.

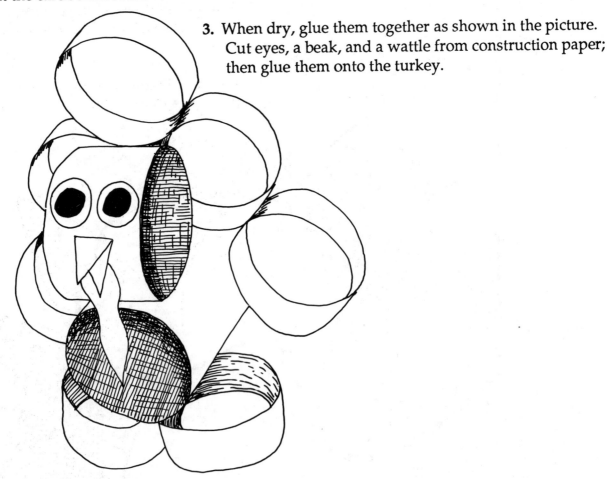

3. When dry, glue them together as shown in the picture. Cut eyes, a beak, and a wattle from construction paper; then glue them onto the turkey.

Turkey Feathers

A variety of materials can be used to easily create eye-appealing turkeys.

Just start with a circle for a simple turkey body. Glue to a construction paper backing. Add a gobbler, head and feet.

Then choose from these "feather ideas" to complete the turkey:

• **"Husky" Feathers** - Glue four or five corn husks (available in produce departments).

• **"Ribbon" Feathers** - Cut shiny ribbon into varying lengths. Loop each ribbon and glue together where ends meet.

• **"Wrapped" Feathers** - Cut feathers from an assortment of gift wrap.

• **"Spongy" Feathers** - Cut sponges in the shape of feathers. Dip and press in a variety of colors.

• **"Fringed" Feathers** - Fringe tissue paper feathers for an "airy" effect.

Alien Turkey

Things You'll Need:

- 12"x18" white construction paper
- plastic spoon
- brown tempera paint, plus assorted colors
- paintbrush

Directions:

1. Fold construction paper in half lengthwise.

2. Unfold and put three dots of paint on the fold. The paint should be evenly spaced and not too close to the ends of the paper.

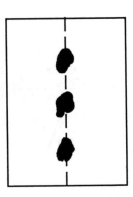

3. Refold the paper carefully. Use the palm of your hand to push the paint out, toward the open sides of the paper. Open and let dry.

4. Paint face, feet and feathers.

Variations:

 Halloween: black paint - monster - add scary features

 Christmas: green paint - free form tree - decorate

 Animals: three colors - invent a new animal

Make a Menorah

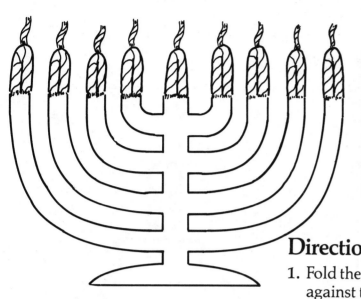

Directions:

1. Fold the brown paper in half. Place the pattern on top against the fold as indicated.
2. Cut out the menorah. Open and glue to blue paper.
3. Glue white yarn candles with orange flames.

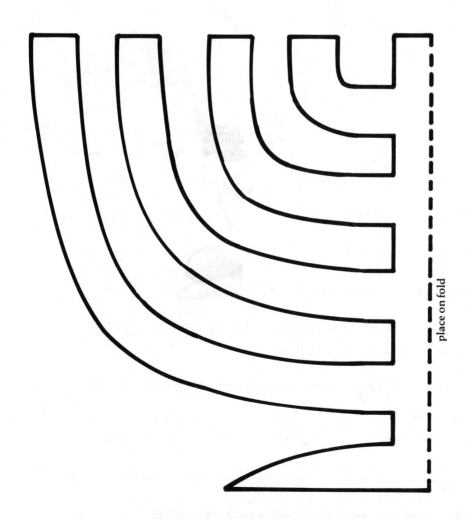

place on fold

RING
in the holidays

Things You'll Need:

- clean plastic containers, any size.
  Save the lid.
- spray paint
- beads, buttons
- felt, ribbon, yarn
- glitter • glue
- hammer, nail

Directions:

1. Wash out bottles and cut off the tops.

2. Spray with paint. Allow to dry.

3. Decorate with glitter, ribbon, yarn or felt.

4. Knot one end of string and thread a button or bead.

5. Make a nail hole in the lid. Thread the yarn through the hole. Leave enough string to hang down from the bell.

Display

Cut out the words: "Ring in the holidays!" or "Ring in the New Year!" Tack the words to a bulletin board. Hang the bells from the ceiling.

PASTA WISEMEN

Things You'll Need:

- assorted macaroni, spaghetti and pasta shapes
- glue • cardboard
- manila construction paper circle
- gold or silver paint (optional)

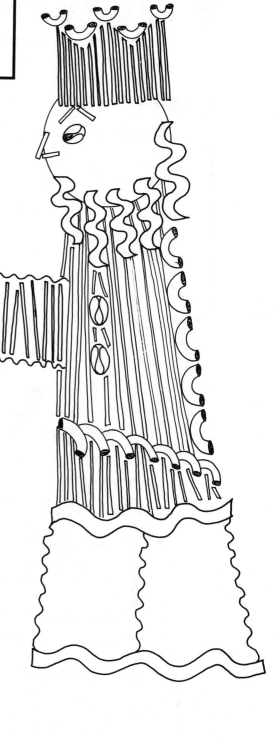

Directions:

1. Glue the circle to cardboard

2. Arrange pasta (breaking if necessary) into wiseman profile.

3. Glue pasta into postion.

4. Paint with gold or silver enamel.

5. Trim cardboard around wiseman.

Display

Recreate a nighttime scene on a wall. Add a bright star in the sky, cut out butcher paper hills. Tack up the wisemen heading toward the star.

(A stable can be added in the distance if you wish.)

Santa on the Move

Things you'll need:

- Santa pattern reproduced on white paper
- 4 brads • cotton balls
- crayons • glue

Directions:

1. Color and cut out the pattern pieces.
2. Match the lettered dots and connect with a brad.
3. Glue cotton on the hat, beard and clothing trim.

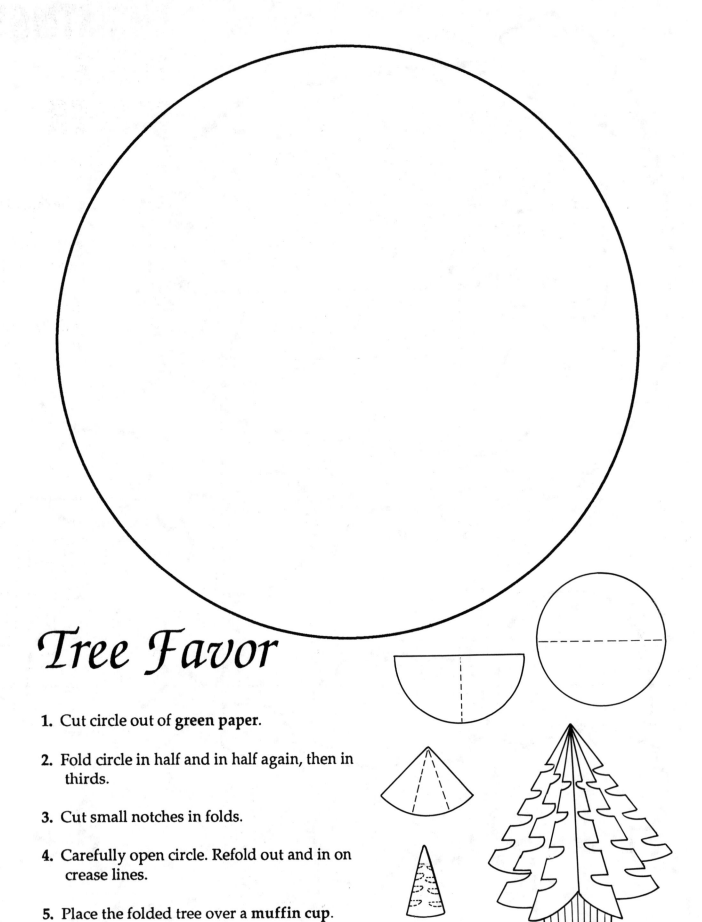

Tree Favor

1. Cut circle out of **green paper**.

2. Fold circle in half and in half again, then in thirds.

3. Cut small notches in folds.

4. Carefully open circle. Refold out and in on crease lines.

5. Place the folded tree over a **muffin cup**.

CHRISTMAS TABLE TOPPER

Color Santa and the chimney.

Cut out along the outside lines.

Fold inward on the lines and glue the tabs inside the box.

Use the small box for favors or notes during the holiday season.

FOLD

FOLD

FOLD

FOLD

ORNAMENT
AVALANCHE

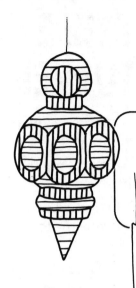

Corrugated Christmas
Cut ornament shapes from corrugated cardboard. Paint with tempera. When dry, brush with a clear lacquer. Hang with thread.

Fancy Circles
Cut three circles from giftwrap, foil, or other paper. Connect them in the center with a brad. Fringe the circles and curl them in different directions. Glue glitter in the center.

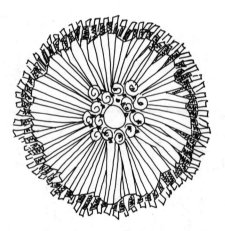

Ribbon Curls
Glue bunches of curling ribbon on construction paper shapes. Hang with a hook.

Rudolph
Cut a reindeer body from construction paper. Add a head. Glue a red tissue ball for a nose.

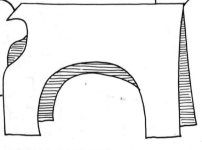

ORNAMENT

Shimmering Shapes

- Start with 2 circles
- Draw a square inside each
- Fold along the lines toward the center
- Cut the same shape out of the center of each
- Tape a piece of gold or silver foil between the two circles and glue them together

Scrolled Ornament

Pour a puddle of glue on a small sheet of waxed paper. Curl folded strips of construction paper around a pencil and press them, sideways, into the glue (see illustration). After the glue dries clear and hard, peel off the waxed paper.

Clothespin Reindeer

Paint an old-fashioned clothespin brown. Add eyes and a bright red nose. Clip to the tree branch.

Pine Cone
Ornaments

Things You'll Need:

- large pine cones
- tempera paint • brush
- glitter • heavy duty shears

Directions:

1. Cut narrow cross sections of pine cone.

2. Paint each petal of the pine cone. Let dry.

3. Paint small shapes in a contrasting color on the pine cone petals.

4. Glue glitter in the center.

5. Poke a hole in one petal and hang with an ornament hook.

Things You'll Need:

- 8 1/2"x11" plain writing paper
- red crayons, marker or paint
- clear tape
- red crepe paper

"Quickie" CANDY CANE

Directions:

1. Paint or color red stripes lengthwise on the writing paper.

2. Roll the paper from one corner, diagonally, to the opposite corner. The tightness of the roll is not important—some canes will be fatter than the others. Tape to hold.

3. Flatten one half. Curl that half around your finger. Let go. If the candy cane shape doesn't hold or look curled enough, curl again.

4. Tie with crepe paper ribbon.

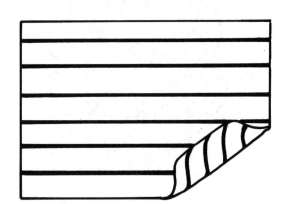

Followup Fun
Creative Writing Topic:
Who paints all the stripes on the candy canes?

Display
Connect the canes with a garland of red or green twisted crepe paper for an appealing border around your classroom.

Tube Santa Claus

Things You'll Need:

- small paper tube
- red, black, pink, white construction paper
- scissors • glue
- cotton

Holiday Help

Santa Claus has many names around the world:

> Père Noel
> Father Christmas
> Saint Nicholas

to name a few. Customs vary but he usually brings small gifts to children on Christmas Eve.

Directions:

1. Cover the tube with red paper.

2. Cut rectangle sleeves, a round face, and glue as illustrated.

3. Cut a red circle to make a cone hat. Trim with cotton.

4. Fringe two layers of white paper for a beard. Glue. Add cotton trim.

It's Raining Reindeer!

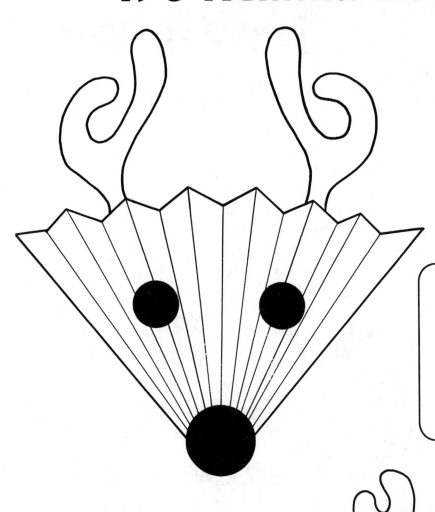

Accordian-fold a square of paper. The size of the square will depend on the finished size you desire.

Cut out and **glue** on eyes, a large red nose and antlers.

Followup Fun

Sing "Rudolph the Red-Nosed Reindeer."

Take turns holding your reindeer in front of your face and act out the words to the song.

Fold a sheet of 6"x9" brown construction paper in half, along the shorter width.

Cut off one end to make it curved.

Add eyes, nose and antlers.

Display

Tack a long piece of bright red yarn in "clothesline" fashion on the wall.

Hang the reindeer along the fold on the yarn.

Things You'll Need:

- large sheet of white construction paper
- half sheet dark green construction paper
- construction paper scraps, assorted colors
- scissors   • stapler
- glue

Folded Fir Tree

Directions:

1. Fan-fold the green paper. Staple the top to hold the shape.
2. Cut slots in the folds. Glue the tree to the white paper.
3. Add a paper trunk.
4. Cut small circles from paper scraps and insert them in the slots.
5. Cut and glue a treetop ornament.

Checkered Christmas Tree

Directions:

1. Reproduce tree pattern on white paper.

2. Reproduce pattern A on red paper.

3. Reproduce pattern B on green paper.

4. Carefully cut around the tree outline. Make one cut starting at the trunk. Save the cut out tree.

5. Cut pattern A out along lines to make five red strips.

6. Fold pattern B on the dotted line. Cut lines from the fold to the *end of the line*. Open and lay flat.

7. Weave red strips through the green.

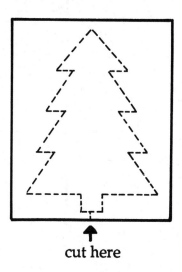

↑
cut here

8. Glue ends in place.

9. Glue white tree to one side of the weaving and the cut out tree to the other side.

10. Hang with yarn.

Variations

Use any of the Quick & Easy Patterns to create holiday or seasonal weavings.

 pink and purple weaving, red heart for **Valentine's Day**

 orange and yellow weaving, black pumpkin for **Halloween**

 blue and yellow weaving, pink egg for **Easter**

blue and green weaving, brown ship for **Columbus Day**.

Pattern A

212

Pattern
B

Heart Holder

Holiday Help

Carry on the tradition of sending a valentine to a loved one. Tuck special notes in this valentine holder.

Things You'll Need:

- 12"x18" white construction paper
- paint • markers • crayons

Directions:

1. Cut one end of the construction paper, as shown.

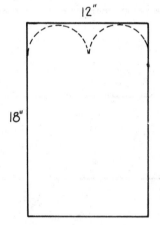

2. Fold up the bottom edge of the paper.

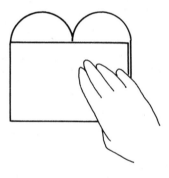

3. Fold each corner toward the center.

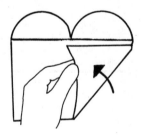

4. Fold down the loose edge and glue in place. Write your name across the glued flap. Decorate with paint, markers and crayons.

"Hearty" Animals

Things You'll Need:

- assorted colors construction paper
- scissors
- glue

Directions:

1. Cut various-sized hearts from construction paper.

2. Assemble them on a larger sheet of paper to create an animal. Hearts can be folded into any shape. Add scraps for features—feathers, eye lashes, tongue, etc.

3. Glue in place.

4. Write a "hearty" animal greeting.

SCROLL OF HEARTS

SUPER BOOK OF ARTS & CRAFTS • *Edupress* • ©1990

THINGS YOU'LL NEED:

- long, narrow strip white butcher paper
- colored construction paper, various colors and sizes
- scissors • glue

DIRECTIONS:

1. Cut as many different kinds and sizes of hearts as you can from the construction paper.

2. Arrange the hearts on the butcher paper. They can be in any direction, overlapping, or on top of each other.

Shamrock Masks

Things you'll need:

- Green construction paper
- shamrock pattern from pattern section
- scissors • glue
- green yarn • marking pens

Directions:

1. Cut a green shamrock using the pattern. (Older children may need to increase the size of the pattern.)
2. Cut holes for eyes.
3. Outline the shamrock with yarn. Use markers to decorate.
4. Attach yarn to each side of the mask to tie around student's head.

Followup Fun

Put on your shamrock mask. Try some role playing.

- Have a conversation with an elf.
- Describe your life in Ireland.
- Make up a story about the "Luck of the Irish." Tell it to your classmates.

SHAMROCKS GALORE!

Color the background one solid color.
Color each shamrock with a different color
or design.

SPROUT A SHAMROCK

Start this project early in March for an extra-green **St. Patrick's Day** celebration.

THINGS YOU'LL NEED:

- small sponge
- shamrock pattern (below)
- grass seed • marking pen
- bowls • water • scissors

HOLIDAY HELP

A shamrock is the national flower of Ireland. According to legend, St. Patrick planted it because its three small leaves represented the Holy Trinity. Many people still wear shamrocks on **St. Patrick's Day.**

DIRECTIONS:

1. Use a marker to trace the pattern on the sponge.

2. Cut out the shamrock shape.

3. Soak the sponge in a bowl of water.

4. Sprinkle heavily with a layer of grass seed.

5. Set in a sunny spot. Check daily and keep the sponge damp.

6. Look for sprouts in about a week.

Here's a fun leprechaun mask for **St. Patrick's Day** role playing and storytelling.

Look Who's a Leprechaun!

Things you'll need:

- one 12" x 18" black construction paper
- one 9" x 12" orange construction paper
- one 9" x 12" green construction paper
- patterns for hat, hair, beard and ears (following pages)
- scissors • glue

Directions:

1. Cut a circle large enough for a child's face out of the center of the black paper.

2. Use the patterns to trace and cut green hat and ears, and orange hair and beard.

3. Glue the cut patterns around the opening in the black paper, as shown in the illustration.

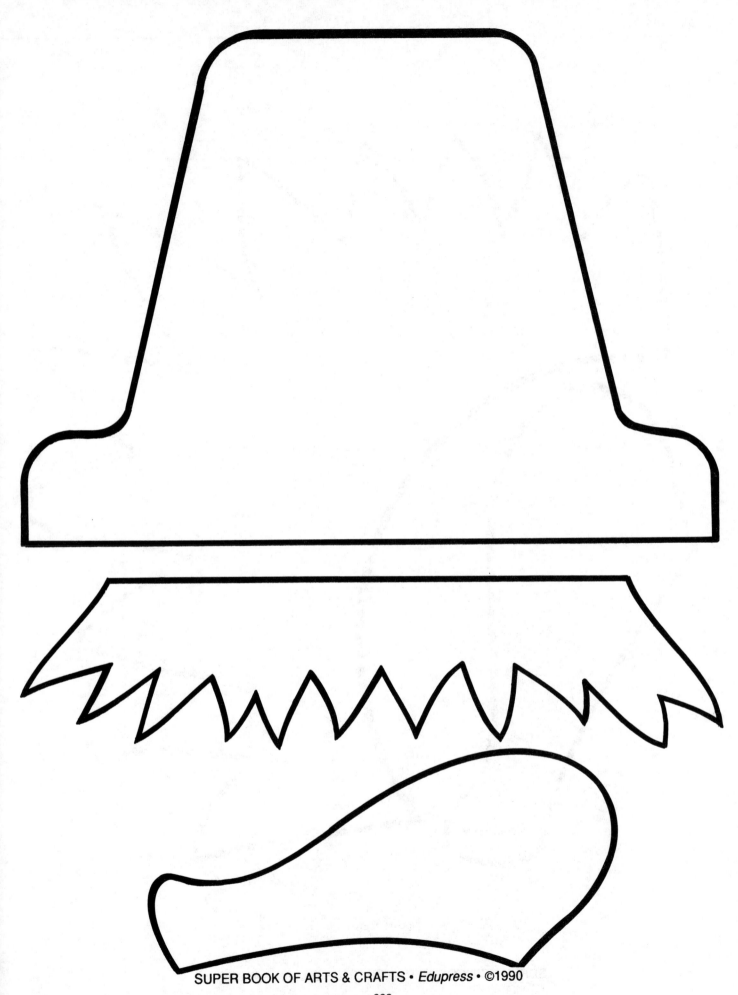

Things You'll Need:

- salt
- water
- liquid starch
- tempera paint
- paintbrush
- paper
- mixing bowls
- small containers

SALTY EGGS

Directions:

1. Prepare salt paint by mixing together four parts salt to one part water and one part starch.
2. Divide the mixture into smaller containers. Stir different colors of tempera paint into each container.
3. Paint some colorful holiday eggs!

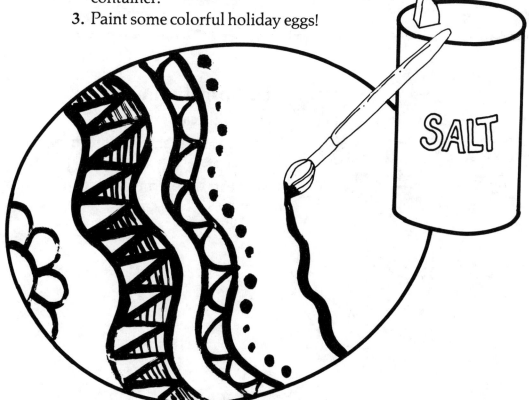

Quick as a "Bunny" Art

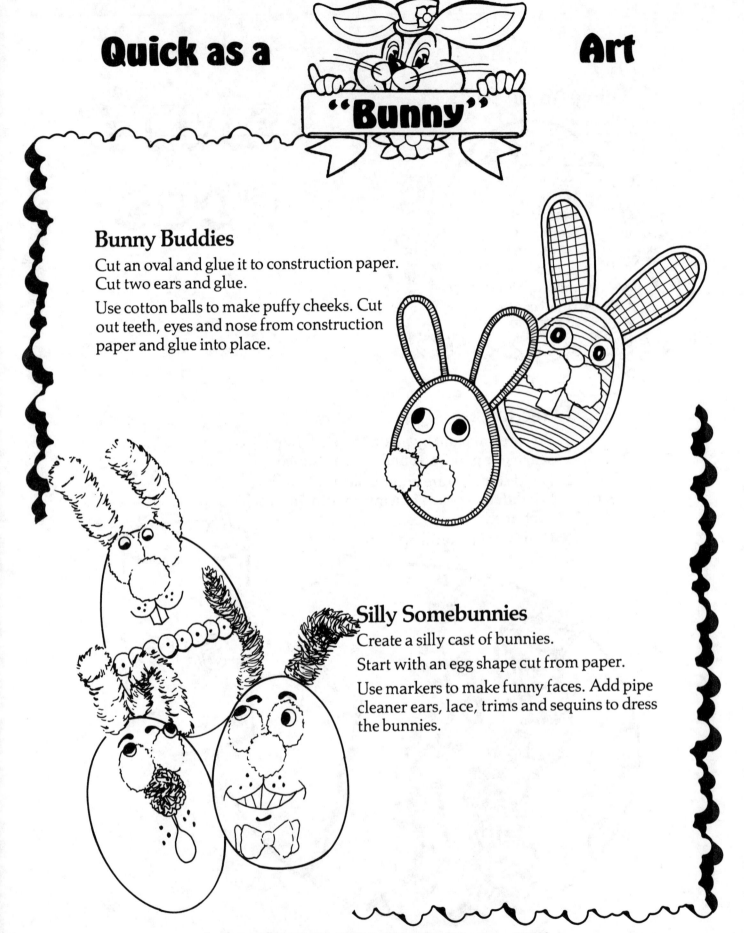

Bunny Buddies

Cut an oval and glue it to construction paper. Cut two ears and glue.

Use cotton balls to make puffy cheeks. Cut out teeth, eyes and nose from construction paper and glue into place.

Silly Somebunnies

Create a silly cast of bunnies.

Start with an egg shape cut from paper.

Use markers to make funny faces. Add pipe cleaner ears, lace, trims and sequins to dress the bunnies.

Easter Party Favor

Things You'll Need:

- white or pink construction paper
- bunny pattern
- one large marshmallow
- cotton ball • glue
- raisins (optional)

1. Trace and cut out bunny parts from   construction paper. Color a face. (Raisins make great eyes.) Glue on a cotton ball tail.
2. Lick two sides of the marshmallow and stick the front of the bunny on one side and the back on the other. (The marshmallow is the center of the bunny.)

Bunny Holder

1. Place the **pattern** on the fold of **white construction paper**. Trace and cut.

2. Decorate front and back with **crayons, watercolors** or **paper**.

3. **Glue** front and back together leaving the area between the ears open and deep enough to poke your finger in.

4. Tuck a **carrot** in the opening for a tasty bunny treat.

Bunny Hop

Color and cut out bunny parts.
Glue to construction paper. Don't
let the pieces touch! Paint or color a
background.

TORN Bunnies

Things You'll Need:

- 12"x18" black construction paper
- white construction paper
- glue   • assorted construction paper scraps

Directions:

1. Tear out a bunny from white construction paper. Glue to the black paper.

2. Add details to the bunny and the background.

Variation

Create any picture using torn paper

 pumpkins   snowmen ❄
monsters   flowers ✿
turkeys

Sponge Bunnies

.....Things You'll Need:........

- 12"x18" dark blue construction paper
- white paint
- sponge • basket grass
- markers, crayons
- cotton balls

Directions:

1. Sponge paint a white bunny on dark blue paper. Don't use too much—the paint should not be solid. Some suggested shapes are:

2. When paint has dried use markers or crayons to add the details. You can use buttons for eyes and cotton balls for a tail.

3. Add a background of basket grass around the bunny.

Gift Grabbag

Need an easy gift idea? Check these pages.

Closet Freshener

- Start with **two** small plain **paper cups**. Use a **nail** to poke holes in both.
- Fill one cup with **potpourri or cloves**. Invert the second cup and glue them together around the lip.
- "Gift wrap" with **yarn or ribbon**, creating a loop at the top for hanging.
- Decorate with **felt scraps**.

Bookmarks

- Fringe a strip of vinyl. Decorate with permanent markers.
- Glue a cardboard cutout to both ends of a ribbon.
- Cut off the corner of an envelope. Decorate and scallop the edges.

Recipe or Memo Holder

- Decorate a plain 2" (5 cm) square tile with permanent markers.

- "Hot" glue a clothespin to the back of the tile. The open end of the clothespin should be even with the edge of the tile. (See illustration.)

Belt or Tie Rack

- Sand a heavy wood hanger until smooth. Paint with designs. Spray with varnish.
- Screw in three to five cup hooks.
- Tie the top with a bow.

Gift Shapes

When finished, these shapes can take a couple forms that make super gifts for any holiday or celebration.

Things You'll Need:
- newspaper
- glue
- scissors
- fine sandpaper
- clear lacquer
- paintbrush
- pattern (from following page or student-designed)
- tempera paint
- index card

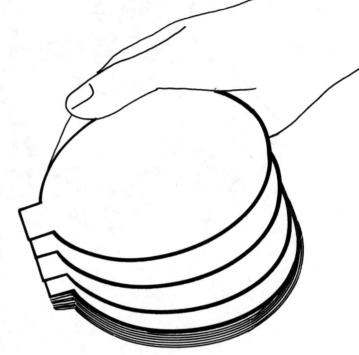

Directions:
1. Choose a shape pattern. Cut a master pattern from an index card.
2. Trace and cut 30 shapes from newspaper. Glue all 30 shapes one on top of the other to create 30 layers.
3. Allow to dry thoroughly.
4. Sandpaper the edges and the sides smooth. Paint with tempera and spray or paint with clear lacquer.

Variations:

Glue a magnet or magnet tape to each shape's back to create a memo holder.

Make a keychain. Before glueing, punch a hole in the top of each shape.

ALL-OCCASION CARDS

Need a card for a special occasion? Here are some ideas that can be adapted to all holidays and celebrations.

Just start with a piece of folded construction paper, decorate and add a personal message.

SHAPE CUT-OUT

❶ Fold the card in half. Cut out half a holiday shape from the front panels as shown.

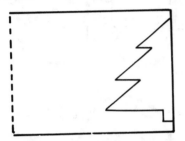

❷ Fold the card in thirds. The cut out shape should meet in the middle.

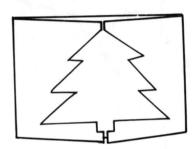

— RECYCLED —

Recycle old cards by cutting off the fronts. Create new cards using parts or all of the original card. Glue in place.

— STENCILED —

Use any holiday shape. Place the stencil shape on the card front. Sponge, splatter paint over the card. Remove the stencil.

— POP-UP —

Glue paper strips to each side of the fold, as shown.

Glue a paper cut out to the paper strip.

Write an appropriate message.

Dip a hand or foot in paint and make a print
on card-folded paper.
Write a cute message and you have a simple,
but lovable message for parents.

Outside message:

THANKS FOR ALWAYS BEING
THERE TO GIVE ME A HAND

Inside message:

WHEN I NEEDED IT MOST

Outside message:

UPON MY SOLE...

Inside message:

I LOVE YOU

Mother's Day Card

Directions:

1. Cut three flower blossoms exactly the same. Cut one flower pot.

2. Fold large paper in half, open and fold both ends to center fold. Open.

3. Glue pieces and write message as shown.

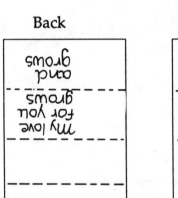

Back — Front

Back:
grows
and
grows
for you
my love

Front:
and
grows

Love,

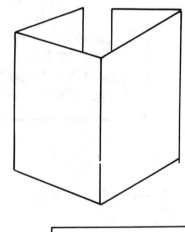

4. Refold card from the top, a section at a time

My love
for you
grows

Love,

and
grows

Love,

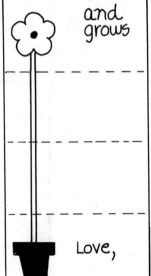

and
grows

Love,

...ther's Day Card

You'll Need:

- white construction paper
- ...l buttons • crayons
- (optional) • scissors

Directions:

1. Fold construction paper in half.

2. Cut two triangle shapes, as shown.

3. Fold the two top corners down so they'll touch, to make a collar.

4. Cut the back collar off, so the card opens easily.

5. Color the shirt to look like one your father wears—striped, Hawaiian, plaid, golf shirt, t-shirt. Add real buttons down the front, and a cloth tie if you want.

6. Write a special message inside.

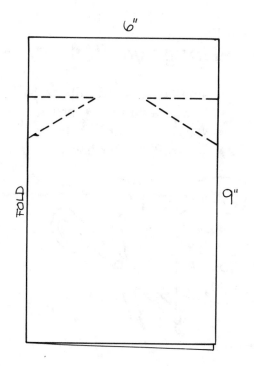

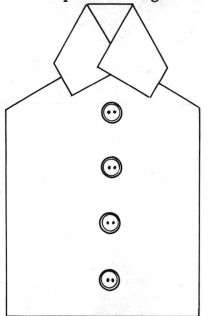

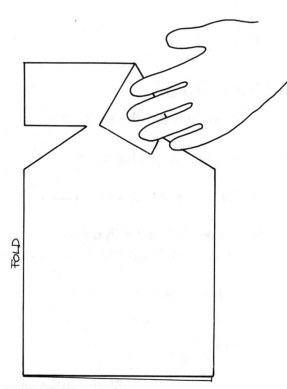

Feathered Friend Feeder

Things you'll need:

- small cardboard milk carton
- tempera paint • brush
- starch • yarn or string
- scissors • birdseed

Directions:

1. Wash and dry the milk carton.

2. Staple the opening closed.

3. Cut out a section of the carton. (See illustration)

4. Poke a hole throuth the top of the container and string yarn or string through to use as a hanger.

5. Fill with birdseed.

Bugs in the Room!

Things You'll Need:

- 6 to 8 bottle caps per student
- gesso
- colored tagboard or chipboard
- construction paper scraps
- felt scraps, pipe cleaners
- glitter, beads
- glue • scissors
- enamel paint   • brush

Directions:

1. Brush bottle caps with a coat of white gesso.

2. Paint bottle caps, any color.

3. When dry, glue the bottle caps in the shape of a bug or insect on tagboard.

4. Use black construction paper, felt and pipe cleaners to add legs, feelers, eyes, antennae, tails and other detail.

5. Glitter or beads can also be used to decorate bugs.

Creature Caddies

Things You'll Need:

- small milk carton
- construction paper
- scissors
- paste or glue

Art Start

Discuss the benefits of keeping a desk organized for better school work and productivity. Then help with this organization by making this desktop holder for pencils, crayons or marker.

Directions:

1. Clean out the milk carton. Cut off the top portion.
2. Cover the outside with construction paper. Glue or tape to hold.
3. Create an animal head. (See illustrations for ideas.) Glue the head to the back of the carton, facing front.
4. Cut feet and/or paws to "match" the animal. Glue them to the front of the carton.

Egg Carton Dragon

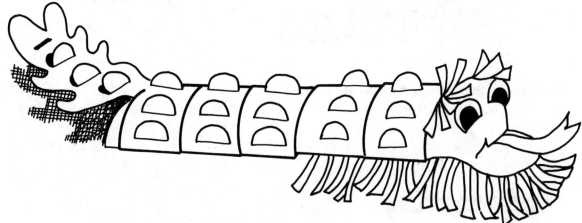

Things You'll Need:

- paper egg carton
- 4 strips green construction paper, 2" (5 cm) x 11" (27.5 cm)
- colored tissue paper or construction paper scraps
- pipe cleaners
- stapler

Directions:

1. Remove the lid from the carton and cut the cup portion in half lengthwise. Cut off a two-cup section and staple it perpendicular to the end of the remaining sections. This will form the dragon's head and mouth.

2. Fold the green paper strips in half lengthwise. Cut curves on the fold (see diagram).

   Open the paper and fold the cut curve up.

3. Wrap the carton with the strips, glueing the strips together under the dragon.

4. Use fringed tissue paper, pipe cleaners, construction paper and other decorations to create detail — tail, tongue, eyes, etc.

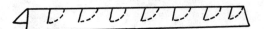 

DECORATED BOTTLES

Fill these bottles with a bouquet of flowers for a special gift or desktop vase.

CORK BOTTLES

Cover a bottle or jar with torn, overlapping pieces of masking tape.

Press the tape firmly to the glass.

Use the rag to apply shoepolish to the tape, rubbing lightly. Spread the polishes as dark or as light as you prefer.

PICTURE BOTTLES

Cut pieces from magazine pictures. Paint the backs with glue and apply the pieces to the bottle in the same overlapping fashion as the project above.

Apply a coat of clear lacquer over the pictures.

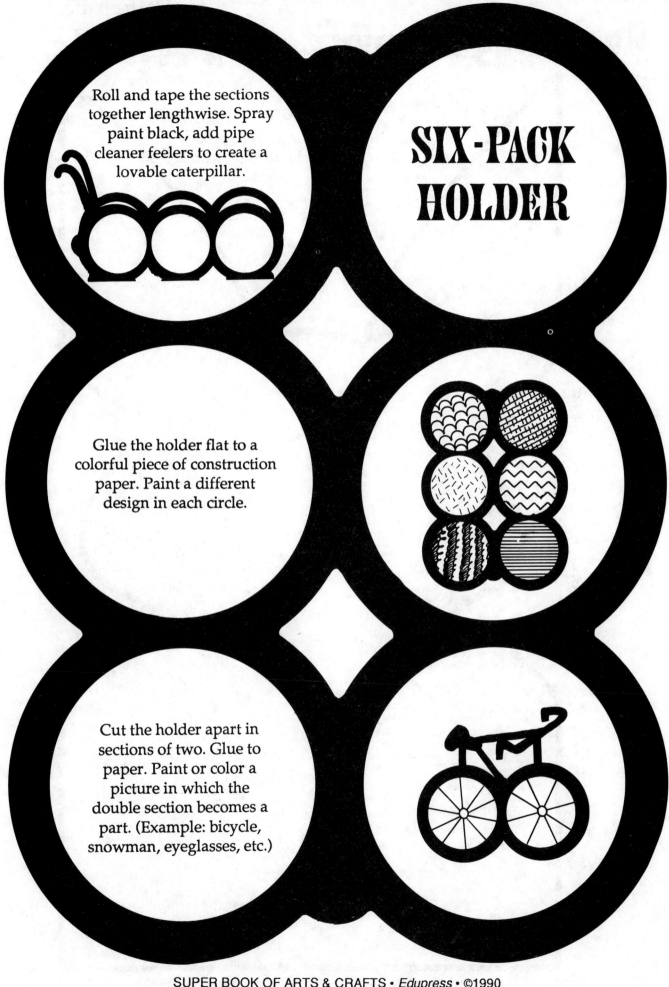

Roll and tape the sections together lengthwise. Spray paint black, add pipe cleaner feelers to create a lovable caterpillar.

SIX-PACK HOLDER

Glue the holder flat to a colorful piece of construction paper. Paint a different design in each circle.

Cut the holder apart in sections of two. Glue to paper. Paint or color a picture in which the double section becomes a part. (Example: bicycle, snowman, eyeglasses, etc.)

Paper Bag Bunnies

Transfer the pattern
to a paper bag.
Decorate both sides.

Variation:

Place pattern on the fold of a piece
of construction paper and make a card.

Bronzed Shoe

Things You'll Need:

- student's old tennis shoe
- waterproof white glue
- bronze or gold spray paint
- small cups for glue
- paintbrush.

Technique Tip

Allow two weeks for this project. Students can add coats of glue to their shoe during free time.

Directions:

1. Paint the shoe inside then out, with glue. DO NOT paint the bottom.

2. Tie the shoelaces in a bow and paint them with glue too.

3. A total of six coats of glue need to be applied to the shoe. Dry thoroughly between each coat.

4. The shoe will increase in hardness between each coat of glue. After the final coat has been applied and is dry, spray or paint with bronze or gold.

Gift Idea

Turn the bronzed shoe into a planter or pencil holder for a special relative or friend.

Followup Fun

How many kids have bronze baby shoes at home? Have them bring them in to share and compare.

JEWELRY JAMBOREE

Jewelry can be used for gift-giving or costumes in a classroom play.
Here are several techniques.

EDIBLE NECKLACES

String **cheerios** on **yarn**. Dip the
tip of the yarn in **glue** first for
easier threading by little hand.

Wear for nutritious snacking
throughout the day.

BUTTON RINGS

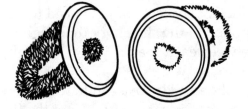

Use a **button** with two holes. Push a
pipe cleaner up through one hole and
back down through the other. Twist
the ends of the pipe cleaner together,
adjusting the ring to the size of your
finger.

COLLAR NECKLACE

Playing the part of an Egyptian
Pharoah? Use a needle and thread
to "sew" **straws** together.

PAPER BEADS

Cut triangles from colorful **magazine** pictures. Roll from the wide end, around a **straw**. **Glue** the point in place. Remove the straw.

Make a necklace, decorate an Indian headdress or create a hair ornament.

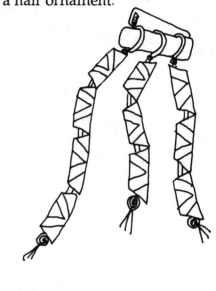

SHIMMERING JEWELRY

Cut out **tagboard** circles large enough to fit over the head, wrist or ankle. Cover with **aluminum foil**. Fold foil shapes in half over the circular frame. Add **bits of paper, sequins**, etc.

Become a prince or princess with a shimmering crown, an Indian with a ceremonial arm or ankle band or a French Poodle with a fancy collar!

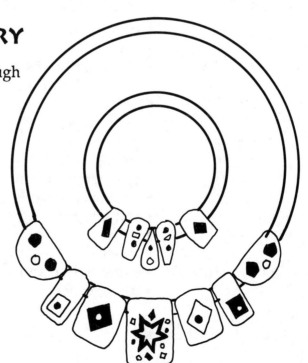

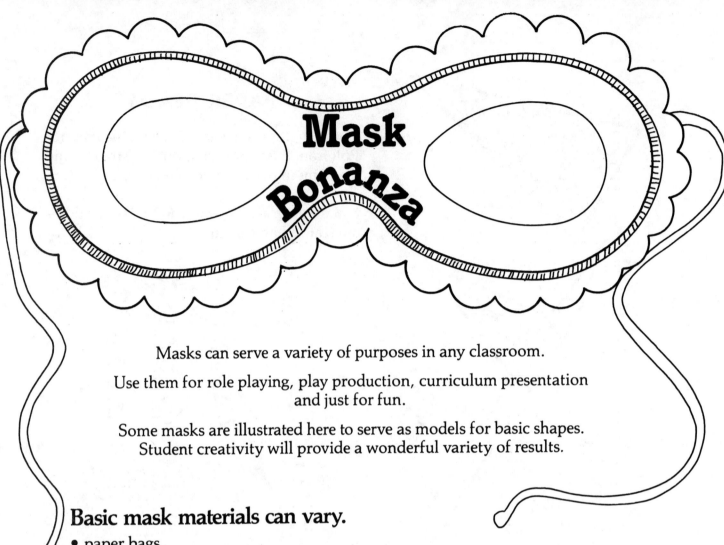

Mask Bonanza

Masks can serve a variety of purposes in any classroom.

Use them for role playing, play production, curriculum presentation and just for fun.

Some masks are illustrated here to serve as models for basic shapes. Student creativity will provide a wonderful variety of results.

Basic mask materials can vary.

- paper bags
- butcher paper
- thin sheets of foam
- tagboard
- construction paper

Decoration ideas are endless:

- styrofoam produce and meat trays cut into shapes
- felt
- sequins, ribbons, feathers, rick-rack, eyelet, costume jewels
- markers, crayons, paints
- raffia
- tissue paper
- paper scraps
- sponge cutouts
- egg carton sections
- baking cups (super for unusual eyes)
- crepe paper
- yarn
- tinsel
- shiny ribbon and press-on bows
- pipe cleaners

Secure the masks with:

- elastic
- yarn or ribbon ties
- rubber bands hooked over the ears and stapled to the mask

Tagboard

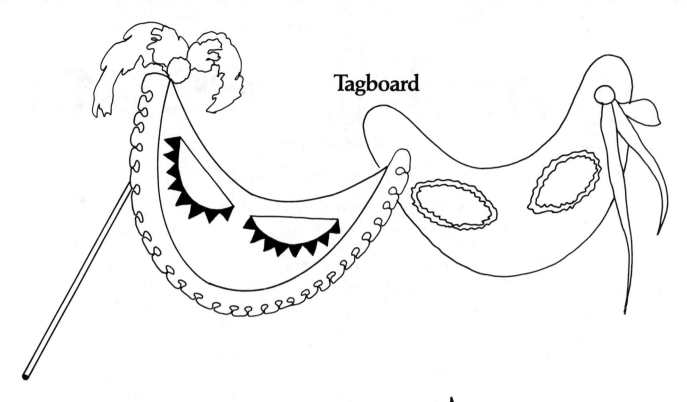

Construction paper and markers

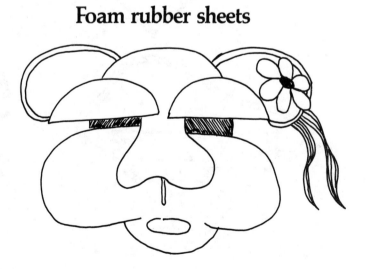

Paper bag

Foam rubber sheets

Card Keeper

Directions:

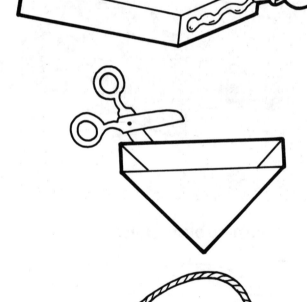

1. Glue the lid to the bottom of the gift box.
2. Following the diagram, cut the corner from the box.
3. Decorate with cut paper shapes. See variations below.
4. Poke a hole at the top of both narrow edges. Tie a piece of yarn and make a knot at each end on the inside of the cardboard.
5. Hang the card keeper from a chair at school . . . ready to receive special notes from special friends!

Variations:

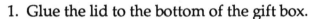

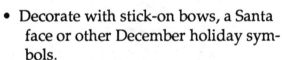

 • Decorate with stick-on bows, a Santa face or other December holiday symbols.

 • Use doilies, hearts and special trims for a super Valentine mailbox.

 • Cover with colorful question marks for notes from secret pals.

• Splash with spring and summer colors for an end of the year letter exchange.

Collection Keepers

Things you'll need:

- 6 plastic ziplock sandwich bags
- two 8" x 8" cardboard or tagboard
- wallpaper, giftwrap or contact paper
- yarn • hole punch • glue

Directions:

1. Cover the tagboard with colorful paper
2. Stack the sandwich bags with the openings all at one end.
3. Place the bags between the tagboard, papered side out. The ziplock opening should run vertically.
4. Punch two holes at the closed ends of the bags.
5. Thread a piece of yarn through each hole and tie in a pretty bow.
6. Collect postcards, stickers, pictures or other special items in your book.

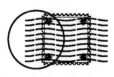

Paper Plate
PUPPETS

Things You'll Need:

- paper plate
- crayons, markers or paint
- assorted art supplies—yarn, construction paper, glue, scissors
- tongue depresser or craft stick
- masking tape

Directions

A paper plate can become any character or holiday symbol with a little imagination and a variety of art supplies.

Create a character or symbol, tape a stick holder to the back then have some puppet fun by making up your own stories and scripts.

Use the puppets for problem solving and role playing, too!

Things You'll Need:

- package of assorted balloons
- yarn or string
- starch and water mixture (3 to 1)
- green pipe cleaner
- green crepe paper
- plaster of paris, creamy mixture
- tempera paint and brushes

Life-like Fruit

Directions:

1. Blow up balloons. Choose ones that look like fruit.

2. Wrap balloon with yarn or string that has been dipped in starch mixture. (It will stick to the balloon easier.)

3. Dip the balloon into a creamy mixture of plaster of paris. Make sure the plaster soaks into the string. Let dry.

4. Paint the fruit with tempera.

5. Add a pipe cleaner stem and crepe paper leaves.

Display

Arrange all fruit in bowls, baskets or bushels for harvest classroom table decorations.

Clay Creations

Self-hardening Clay Dough

Mix together in a large bowl:

1 cup (500 ml) all-purpose flour
1/2 cup (250 ml) salt

Add 1/3 cup (166 ml) of water a little at a time. Squeeze the dough with your hands until it is smooth.

Technique Tip

Work on a sheet of waxed paper to prevent sticking. Paint with acrylics after hardened and dry.

Brush with clear nail polish to finish.

Clay Animals

Snake

Roll clay into long rope. Use a paper clip to make scales. Shape into a slithery snake.

Snail

Roll clay into a thick rope. Roll into a coil. Add toothpick antennae. Paint.

Dinosaur

Start with an oval chunk of clay. Flatten small pieces of clay and mold to the body part to create horns, scales, feet.

Use small beads pressed into clay for eyes.

More Clay Creations

Beads

Make assorted shapes: small balls, flat squares or circles, rounded ovals.

Use a nail to make a hole through the center of each shape.

Make keychains, wall hangings or jewelry.

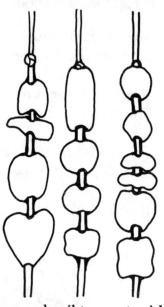

Baskets

Flatten a circle of clay for the base. Roll clay ropes and coil to create sides.

Poke holes for a handle. Add a clay or pipe cleaner handle.

Decorate with a ribbon on the handle.

Menorah

Roll 8 balls of clay. Connect them side by side. Roll one larger ball and connect it to the end. Use your thumb to make an indentation large enough to hold a candle. Dry and paint.

Basic Bread Dough

2 cups (1,000 ml) flour
1 cup (500 ml) salt
1 cup (500 ml) water

Mix the flour and salt together in a large bowl. Slowly add the water while mixing until the dry ingredients are uniformly moistened.

Remove the mixture from the bowl and knead for 6 to 10 minutes on a well-floured surface.

Choose from the project menu. Bake dough at 325 degrees. Baking times will vary depending upon the size of the object.

If you want to have a golden color, brush with egg white prior to baking.

Technique Tips

Do not use self rising flour. If dough is too dry, add water. If puffiness occurs while baking, prick with a toothpick.

Practically any paints can be used to color projects after baking. Food colorings tend to fade when baked.

All projects should be preserved by spraying with clear sealer.

Project Menu

Ornaments—Insert an ornament hook through the top before baking.

Jar lids—Cover the lid of the jar. Add dough cut outs. Bake. Fill the jar with homemade goodies.

Sweetheart Pin—Use a heart-shaped cookie cutter, bake, add a pin backing.

Memo Magnet—Press a magnetic strip on the back before baking.

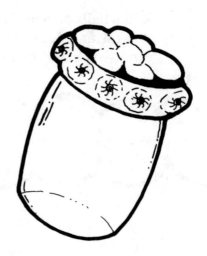

Makeup Magic

Here's a living art project. Follow the recipe, then take turns making up classmates.
The face is your canvas!

Makeup

Mix together:

facial cleansing cream (2 tablespoons)
flour or cornstarch (1 tablespoon)
a couple drops of water
food coloring

Technique Tip

Fingers and brushes may be used to apply makeup. Keep containers of water and rolls of paper towels ready. Encourage kids to experiment—if they aren't satisfied with their "creations" the canvas is easily cleaned!

Followup Fun

Plan a "dress up" day in class. Ask kids to bring in simple costumes for roleplaying.

Dress up, make up, and have a ball!

ACTION ART

Magic Lava

1/2 cup (250 ml) cornstarch
1/2 cup (250 ml) water
5 drops food coloring

Mix all ingredients together.

Make a ball out of the "lava" by holding it in a tightly clenched fist. Relax your hand. The lava will "melt" and run. It will harden again if clenched and squeezed into ball.

Store lava in a small margarine tub with the lid tightly sealed.

Bubble Recipe

2 cups warm water
6 tablespoons glycerine (available at drugstores)
6 tablespoons liquid soap
food coloring

Mix all ingredients with a wire whisk or hand held beater. Make several batches of different colors.

Use bubble blowers, straws or bent wire for windy day fun. Even clean tin cans (with both ends removed) will make super giant bubbles!

"Catch" the bubbles on paper, in plastic cups or in your hands. Clean up is easy!

Java BATIK

Here is a simplified classroom version of Batik.

ARTISTIC FACTS

Batik is a method of applying colored designs to fabric. The word and the method come from **Java**.

A design is made with paraffin. When dipped into dye, the wax resists the dye. then the wax is removed by boiling the cloth.

THINGS YOU'LL NEED:

- 9" x 12" **manila** paper
- crayons
- black tempera paint
- paintbrush

DIRECTIONS:

1. Create a patchwork design on the manila paper.

2. Color each section heavily using lines and complimentary colors, i.e. purple/blue, orange/yellow, pink/red.

3. Crush the paper into a ball, open carefully and flatten.

4. Paint the design with a black tempera wash.

5. Lightly blot the paint.

DISPLAY:

To make a picture frame fold a 9" x 12" piece of construction paper in half. Measure 1" around the outside and cut out center, beginning at the folded edge. Open and glue to batik design.

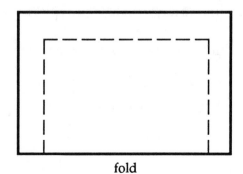

fold

Masks & MORE Masks

ARTISTIC FACT

Masks, in a variety of shapes and colors, are worn throughout the world during the celebration of carnivals, festivals and religious ceremonies.

Masks are made from all kinds of materials—paper, cloth, grass, bark, hide, leather, metal and shell among them.

ART START

Look through books for pictures of masks from different countries.

Make a class scrapbook of the masks you find. Kids can color their own pictures from books and encyclopedias to add to the scrapbook.

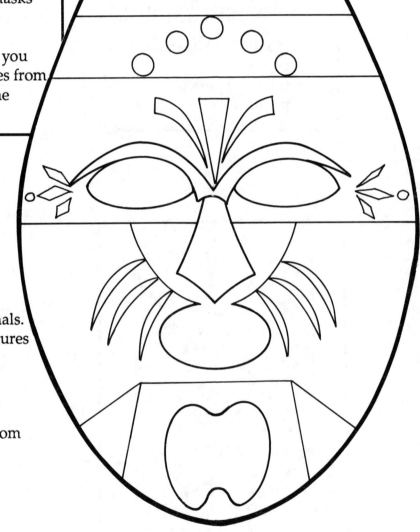

GREEK THEATRICAL MASK

Worn by actors in the theatre, these masks represented a variety of characters or animals. The shape was the same for all but the features were changed to suit the character.

DIRECTIONS:

1. Cut the shape as shown at right from tagboard or construction paper.

2. Cut an oval mouth opening.

3. Color brightly.

Masks & MORE Masks

African Ceremonial Mask

Things You'll Need:
- tagboard
- pencil • scissors
- watercolors, brish
- hole punch
- stapler
- raffia or yarn

Directions

1. Cut mask shape from tagboard

2. Sketch a face or design. Paint with bright watercolors.

3. Cut around the nose area and bend forward.

4. Cut a geometric shape from tagboard or construction paper and staple to the top as shown.

5. Punch holes around the mask edges. Tie with strips of yarn or raffia.

Technique Tip

For a nice finish on the yarn or raffia, fold the length in half. Poke the looped end through the hole. Put open ends through the loop and pull tight.

Brazilian Carnival Mask

Masks
& MORE
Masks

┌─ **Things You'll Need:** ─┐
- bleach (slightly diluted)
- cotton swabs
- 9"x12" colored construction paper (no dark colors)
- black crayon   • scissors

This is a project for older children. Caution them on the dangers of bleach.

Directions:

1. Dip the cotton swab in the diluted bleach. Use the swab like a pencil; draw the outline of a "face" on the construction paper. Any shape will work. See the illustrations above for ideas.

2. Sketch facial features. The more abstract the better.

3. Bleach out some areas of the mask or fill with heavily-colored black crayon.

4. To create a dimensional effect, clip masks at top and bottom, overlap and staple to hold.

┌─ **Technique Tip** ─┐
Dip the swab frequently in the bleach mixture for best results.

INDIA RANGOLI

ARTISTIC FACT

To celebrate many occasions, Indian mothers decorate the floor of their homes. As a youngster, a girl learns the art from her mother.

Rangoli is done by letting rice flour mixed with water slip from between the fingers. It takes practice to learn how. Brushes are not used.

These designs are not meant to last. They wear out in a few days.

THINGS YOU'LL NEED:

- flour
- several tubs or bowls for mixing
- linoleum squares **or** waxed paper

DIRECTIONS:

1. Make a very thin mixture of flour and water in large tubs.

2. Seat small groups of children around each tub. If possible, get old squares of linoleum from a flooring store for the project. Otherwise, work over sheets of waxed paper.

3. Just have fun with this project. Let the mixture slip through your fingers and onto the paper or flooring.

4. When dry, use fingers to paint with watercolors.

Japan Carp Kite

Artistic Fact

The chinese, Japanese, Koreans and Malayans have made interesting kites for hundreds of years.

Kiteflying is an important part of the Boys' Festival held on May 5 in Japan and on Kites' Day, the ninth day of the ninth month in China.

On those days, thousands of kites shaped like dragons, fish, birds and butterflies fly over the cities and towns.

The symbol of courage, a carp kite is flown for every boy in a Japanese family.

To make a carp kite, cut two exact shapes from butcher paper.

Decorate both sides, stuff lightly with newspaper. Staple together around the edges. Leave mouth open.

Attach string to the mouth opening.

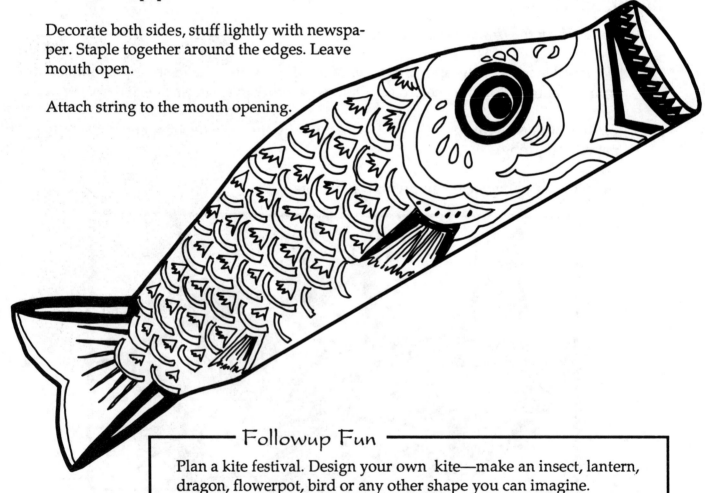

Followup Fun

Plan a kite festival. Design your own kite—make an insect, lantern, dragon, flowerpot, bird or any other shape you can imagine.

Art Around the World

CHINA DRAGON SCROLLS

THINGS YOU'LL NEED:

- long narrow piece of butcher paper
- glue mixed with black tempera paint
- pencil
- colored chalk

DIRECTIONS:

1. Sketch a large dragon on the butcher paper. Color with chalk.

2. Outline all parts of the dragon with the paint/ glue mixture. Allow to dry.

3. Roll and tie with a ribbon.

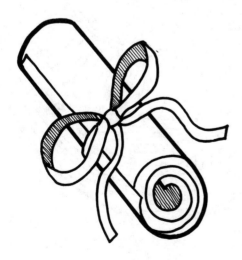

MEXICO MIRROR PLATE

Here's a colorrful accent mirror made by our neighbors in Mexico.

THINGS YOU'LL NEED:
- oval cardboard
- aluminum foil
- scissors • glue
- yarn, assorted thickness and colors

DIRECTIONS:

1. Glue a large piece of aluminum foil to the center of the cardboard.

2. Leaving an oval-shaped section of foil exposed in the center, cover the rest of the cardboard with yarn. Spread the glue in a thin layer then press yarn into place. Vary the direction, colors and widths of yarn used.

   If you wish to hang the mirror, glue the top of a pop-top aluminum can to the back.

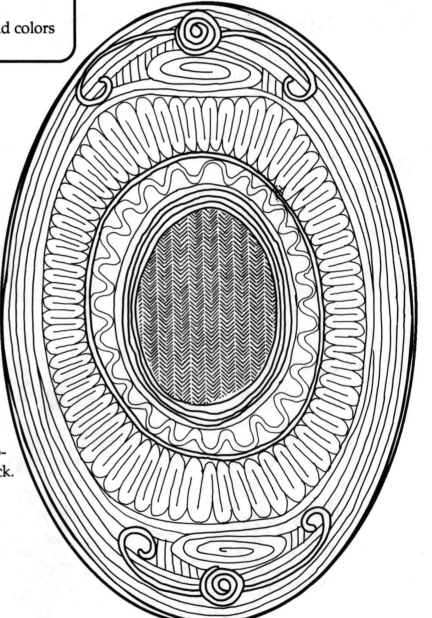

PHILIPPINES WIND CHIMES

THINGS YOU'LL NEED:

- aluminum cans
- stick
- yarn • scissors
- permanent markers

FOLLOWUP FUN

Imagine you're relaxing on this island, the trade winds gently blowing the wind chimes next to your chair!

DIRECTIONS:

1. Cut open the aluminum cans. Cut six circles exactly the same size.

NOTE: The cans are extremely safe and cut with ordinary scissors.

2. Decorate each circle using permanent markers. You can make a design or a picture.

3. Punch a hole in the top of each circle. Tie a knot at each hole and hang on the dowel, as illustrated.

Australia Bark Painting

Artistic Fact

Aborigine tribes in Australia use bark stripped from trees as a "canvas" for their primitive painting.

Things You'll Need:

- brown paper bag
- colored chalk
- black crayon
- masking tape
- brown watercolors, brush

Directions:

1. Tear bag into any shape.

2. Tear small pieces of masking tape and scatter around the paper.

3. Outline a design with black crayon.

4. Color the spaces with chalk.

5. Crumple the paper. Brush lightly with brown paint.

INDEX

W

Y